D0002009

THE BAPTIST MINISTRY
THEN AND NOW

THE

BAPTIST

MINISTRY

THEN AND NOW

By
ROBERT G. TORBET

Foreword by
LYNN LEAVENWORTH

PHILADELPHIA

CHICAGO   THE JUDSON PRESS   LOS ANGELES

KANSAS CITY   SEATTLE

Library of Congress Catalog Card No. 53-6776

PRINTED IN THE U.S.A.

Table of Contents

Foreword

THE COMMISSION ON THE MINISTRY of the American Baptist Convention is acutely aware of the need for a study of the nature and function of the Baptist ministry. There is, at this mid-point of the Twentieth Century, a widespread concern and activity in the area of church leadership development. Foundational studies are needed to provide both laymen and pastors with a perspective for understanding the current projects in In-Service Training, Conferences on the Ministry, Ordination Standards, Placement Procedures, Minimum Salary Plans, and the like. Enthusiasm and purpose can find effectiveness and power only through the establishment of basic understanding.

Dr. Robert G. Torbet, as an observant and competent historian, was encouraged to produce the present study to fill this felt need. Such encouragement has come from Dr. Luther Wesley Smith, Executive Secretary of the Board of Education and Publication; Dr. Milton C. Froyd, who with Dr. Hugh Hartshorne produced the widely influential analysis of the present-day Baptist ministry; and by other leaders connected with the Department of Theological Education and the Commission on the Ministry.

After an examination of the study it has been felt genuinely that it can give individuals and groups across the country the needed basic historical perspective. The work is bound to stimulate a deeper appreciation of our rich Baptist heritage and a moving sense of responsibility for our present and future.

Specifically, it is hoped that state and national committees concerned with the development of leadership will avail themselves of this significant material. It is further hoped that such committees will actively promote the use of the study as a basic

7

text for study at assemblies, conferences, and local church groups.

Beyond all of this, it is our deepest prayer that this book may be used by Baptist men and women everywhere to gain deeper understandings, clearer vision, and more resolute determination as together we move toward a more effective witness to Christ through our Baptist churches.

LYNN LEAVENWORTH

Director, Department of Theological Education
The Board of Education and Publication of
the American Baptist Convention

CHAPTER I

The Beginnings of a Ministry

THIS IS the story of the Baptist ministry during the past three and a half centuries. The period of European and British beginnings will be portrayed briefly, for the main emphasis is to be upon American church life. This emphasis can be justified, because the majority of the readers of this book will be Baptists of the United States and because the greater proportion of Baptist membership is American.

It is hoped that several purposes will be fulfilled by these pages. Their mission is, first of all, to trace briefly the rise of a ministry among "the people called Baptists," and to point out the place and achievements of Baptist ministers in the ever-changing scenes of our church life. A second purpose is to provide a historical perspective for evaluating the concept and practice of selection, ordination, and placement of ministers by Baptist churches. A third purpose, no less important because mentioned last, is to show the importance of a trained ministry and to give some account of the efforts in recent years to elevate the standards for the ministry.

It has been said facetiously, yet with much truth, that the Protestant Reformation did not so much unfrock the clergy as it ordained the laity. What the quipster meant was that the Reformers did not confine the true church to those who had entered Holy Orders, but taught that it embraced every person who had committed himself to devoted discipleship in the name of Jesus Christ. This view, quite naturally, was a reaction against an institutionalized type of Christianity which maintained rigid lines of demarcation between priests and people, between Holy Orders and general communicants, between the truly spiritual believers and the carnal believers.

More consistently than some and certainly more emphatically than others, Baptists have always insisted that, because the New Testament church was a fellowship of confessing disciples, it is

9

the responsibility of every believer to witness. An ordained ministry differs from the rank and file of Christians, not in quality of life, but in degree of function. The minister, therefore, is committed to the apostolic task of preaching the good news and to the pastoral task of instructing in Christian truth and of training in Christian worship. The ordained minister is in the "apostolic succession" only in the sense that it includes all believers who have seen and responded to "the need of the world," the call of Christ, and the tradition of his ministry in the flesh in Galilee and Judea and in the Church which is his Body throughout the world." [1]

Thus, a settled ministry, in the New Testament meaning of the term and in accordance with the pattern followed therefrom by Baptists, was a kind of service needed to lead men to Christ and to develop them in Christian living. It did not require either full-time duty or remuneration, or special academic degrees, although such were not to be despised. The primary essentials in all cases was a call of God to proclaim the good tidings of the Kingdom and a reasonable ability to fulfill the responsibilities of a faithful witness to a personal and vital experience with Christ.

The first-century pattern of a settled ministry, with its variety of expressions through the apostles, the presbyters, and the overseers (or bishops), was destined to become more rigidly settled ecclesiastically during the second century. Soon after the passing of the apostles, the frightening experiences of the early church, torn by heresies, rent by schisms, and shaken by persecutions, gave rise to the investment of increased authority in the office of the overseers or bishops. Whether justified or not, this move was fraught with grave consequences.

Although it is not possible to trace here the gradual rise of the bishop's authority over laymen and priests alike (accompanied as it was by a special recognition of certain primates or chief bishops in the metropolitan cities of the East and at Rome in the West), we need to recognize that this trend was part of the development of an institutional type of Christianity. It was an expression of church life which would confine the flow of the grace of God to believers through a special channel;

[1] T. W. Manson, *The Church's Ministry* (Philadelphia, 1948), pp. 55-56.

namely, the ordained clergy, by whose divine office were dispensed the sacraments of the church. In fact, it was the intrusion of a sacramental view of the church as the extension of the incarnation of our Lord which provided the theological justification for insisting upon forms, ceremonies, and a closely knit organization known as the priesthood for dispensing God's grace to men.

The logical conclusion of such thinking about the importance of the externals of the church to its proper functioning was the extremely hardened form of sacramentalism and ecclesiasticism which characterized the Medieval Church under its monarchial head, the Pope at Rome. It is significant, indeed, that the Medieval Period (from the eleventh to the fourteenth centuries) which saw the fruition of this trend, witnessed also the rise of protest groups, such as the Waldensians, the Petrobrusians, the Henricians, the Lollards, and the Hussites—all of whom rebelled against the control of the church by the priests. In fact, all of these reform sects were laymen's efforts to share in the spiritual life of the church. Most of them insisted that every believer had a responsibility to witness and that holiness was required of all Christians. But alas! the papacy would not listen. So the Reformation of the sixteenth century became an open revolt and protest against an institution which had kept the Bible and the free life of the Spirit away from the rank and file of men and women.

Out of the spirit of nonconformity which thus expressed itself in opposition to the preponderance of forms over the free life of the Spirit, there came a conception of the church and of the ministry which was more nearly like that of the New Testament teaching. It included an insistence upon the necessity of personal decision as the basis of salvation and membership in the church. It viewed the church as a community of the regenerate "gathered" from the world. To be sure, such teaching was not held consistently, not even by all who bore the name of Protestant. The Lutherans, for example, went only part way in breaking with the medieval pattern: they continued a state church connection. Likewise, the Calvinists did not go all the way in rejecting the formal and institutional character of the church. And the Episcopalians continued without serious

12 BAPTIST MINISTRY: THEN AND NOW

change the Catholic practice of sacramentalism and formalism in church life.

Those who most clearly and consistently applied the New Testament principles to their church life were the Anabaptists (called Mennonites today) and the English Baptists, who followed their example in the seventeenth century. These groups taught that the church is a priesthood of believers, with no separated order of priests. The endowment of an individual with special gifts of the Spirit determines his ministry. Therefore, the ministry is a company of men or women who have been called, endued with power, and set apart by God for a special office in the church. The recognition of this office by the church is called "ordination." As a great English Baptist put it, "The office grew out of the gift, and not vice versa." [2]

Baptists see no justification on the basis of New Testament evidence for a marked distinction of privilege and status between clergy and laity. The difference is merely one of function and service. Hence, it is quite proper to say that a ministry of laymen and a ministry of clergy do not differ in nature, but only in kind. This was perhaps one of the most creative insights of the entire Reformation. Furthermore, it opened to laymen an unparalleled opportunity for expression and service in the centuries that followed.[3] Henceforth, divine calling was not exclusively for a priestly class. The concept of a Christian vocation was now applied to farmers, artisans, tradesmen, lawyers, doctors, and housewives. When properly understood and applied, this principle was revolutionary in church life. Indeed, its full effectiveness is yet to be realized.

This concept of the ministry influenced Baptist church life in England, which in turn influenced the pattern in America. In the first place, the selection and ordination of a likely candidate for the ministry were in the hands of the congregation, and not reserved to the order of bishops as in the Episcopalian or Catholic Churches, nor to the elders as in the Presbyterian and Reformed Churches. This practice, in itself, gave recognition to the role of laymen in church affairs. It placed responsibility

[2] H. Wheeler Robinson, *The Life and Faith of the Baptists* (London, 1946), p. 102.

[3] Hugh Hartshorne and Milton C. Froyd, *Theological Education in the Northern Baptist Convention* (Philadelphia, 1945), p. 21.

with the company of believers, godly men and women, on the strength of a conference in their judgment and capacity for leadership under the guidance of the Holy Spirit.

Not infrequently a young man would find his way into the ministry because some kindly minister or friend had recognized certain gifts of speech and spiritual power which he possessed. Such was the case of Samuel Pearce, who played an important part with William Carey and Andrew Fuller in the formation of the Baptist Missionary Society at Kettering in 1792. Pearce was the son of a silversmith in Plymouth, England. His home training and church background were strongly Baptist. At the age of seventeen he was converted under the influence of a student from Bristol College who had been supplying in his parents' church with a view to being called as assistant minister. Very soon thereafter, Pearce's pastor and some friends in the church saw in him possibilities for the ministry:

Something marked him out at once as of unusual spiritual power. The calm countenance, framed in dark brown hair, the sensitive mouth, the brown beaming eyes, the ready speech, the obvious sincerity, combined to give his friends confidence in him, and to make them desire that he should be trained for the ministry.[4]

He was made a probationer. In November, 1783, less than three years later, he received a call to a church as lay preacher. Then he went to Bristol College for training. In 1789 he was called to the Cannon Street Baptist Church in Birmingham. He was ordained in 1790.[5]

In the seventeenth century, ordination procedure among Baptists was not without some confusion. Baptists were concerned lest, by their practice of ordination, they give the impression of violating their basic concept of the ministry. Yet they recognized the New Testament practice of setting aside "gifted brethren" for special service by a laying on of hands by the elders. But even when so performed, there was danger that a person might interpret his ordination as endowing him with an authority beyond the right of his office. Accordingly, some churches eliminated the ceremony entirely; they simply recognized by

[4] Ernest A. Payne, *The First Generation* (London, 1936), p. 48.
[5] Andrew Fuller, *Memoirs of the Late Rev. Samuel Pearce, A.M.,* in *The Baptist Library: A Republication of Standard Baptist Works* (New York, 1855), pp. 341-43.

the "imposition of hands" upon the minister the call by a congregation and his acceptance of it. This was regarded as "confirmation of the ordination that was inherent in the call and its acceptance. Furthermore, this ordination was considered valid only for that church." [6]

Other churches went so far as to "lay hands" upon all believers who came into church membership. This ceremony, following immediately upon baptism, was an indication of the enduement of the individual by the Holy Spirit. In other words, all believers were looked upon as *called* in a general sense. The presence or absence of certain recognized gifts or abilities would determine whether the individual's call was to be a minister. There were yet other Baptists who recognized the validity of an ordination ceremony for setting apart a man for the ministry; in their view, the service was valid only for the pastorate to which he had been called.

The development of a prepared ministry in those days of Baptist beginnings in England depended largely upon the insights and determination of individual ministers. Fortunately many of these men had come into Baptist leadership from a background of the Church of England, Presbyterianism, or Independency (Congregationalism). They had received good training and appreciated its value for the ministry. Dr. John Sutcliff, pastor at Olney for thirty-nine years, and known as "father of the Baptist Missionary Society," was reared under that influence. So earnestly did he value education that when still a youth under twenty, he walked in midwinter from his home in Yorkshire to Bristol College—a week's journey over roads infested with highwaymen. It is little wonder that later in life he gave diligent care to William Robinson, a young boy who wanted to be a foreign missionary. Knowing that the lad was subject to fits of depression and temper, Dr. Sutcliff first gave him personal training and counsel, then sponsored him before the Committee of the Baptist Missionary Society.[7]

But the rank and file of early Baptists were not so concerned with education. Only a minority were alert to the need of a trained ministry. Consequently, their ministers were poorly

[6] Hartshorne and Froyd, *op. cit.*, p. 25.
[7] Payne, *op. cit.*, pp. 40, 106.

paid, and many of them were forced to supplement their meager income by keeping schools. Particular (or Calvinistic) Baptists were especially loath to strengthen their work through organization. Underwood says that "they clung to the independency they had inherited from the Separatists out of whom they had sprung, and they made almost a fetish of the autonomy of the local congregation." [8]

When the first Assembly of Particular Baptists was called to meet at London in September, 1689, by Kiffin, Knollys, Keach, and four other ministers, one of the purposes suggested was that they give "fit and proper encouragement for the raising up of an able and honorable ministry for the time to come." To its credit, be it said that the Assembly established a fund to assist weak churches to support their ministers, to send preachers to unevangelized areas, and to aid ministerial candidates "in attaining a knowledge of Latin, Greek, and Hebrew." [9] Although we may not regard the curriculum of studies as being adequate, it was a step in the right direction.

In 1679 the will of Edward Terrill, a writing master at Bristol and an elder of the Broadmead Church, left a bequest that became in 1720 the foundation of what is today Bristol Baptist College. In 1717 the London Particular Baptists established a fund to train ministerial candidates and to assist needy ministers. In 1804 John Fawcett, an able Baptist minister, became one of the founders of Horton Academy (now Rawdon College), established to train leaders for the churches of Yorkshire and Lancashire.

And so we might continue, if there were space, the story of Baptist educational progress in England. Let it suffice to conclude this brief background survey with a cryptic remark made by the great Charles Haddon Spurgeon, whose college for the training of pastors was established in 1856.

To the objection that too many men were being trained and that some were of inferior quality, Spurgeon replied: "The muffs are the men who will preach; if you do not educate them, they will be worse than ever."[10]

[8] A. C. Underwood, *A History of the English Baptists* (London, 1947), pp. 128-29.

[9] *Ibid.*, p. 129.

[10] *Ibid.*, p. 222.

By the time of his death, his college alone had trained nearly nine hundred men for the ministry. English Baptists had come a long way in a little less than three centuries. Today the *Baptist Handbook* of the Baptist Union of Great Britain and Ireland lists as duly accredited ministers those who have had a divine call, who serve a Baptist church, and who have fulfilled a prescribed course of study at a theological college or its equivalent, with some practical experience in the ministry during a probationary period.[11]

QUESTIONS FOR DISCUSSION

1. In what ways did early Baptists seek to develop a ministry which was true to the spirit of the New Testament?

2. How were early Baptist ministers discovered and ordained?

3. How effective were the minority of early Baptists who were concerned about an educated ministry?

PROJECT SUGGESTIONS

1. Begin a *Notebook of Facts,* in which you can put from time to time such information as will identify the following terms and names: clergy, laity, ordination, Samuel Pearce, Bristol College, Charles Haddon Spurgeon.

2. Write a one-hundred-word essay on the subject, "What Constitutes a Call to the Ministry?"

[11] Robinson, *op. cit.,* p. 105.

CHAPTER II

The Baptist Ministry in Early America

THEY WERE a disturbing element—those first Baptist ministers in colonial America. That is not strange, for they had come from a goodly company of nonconformists abroad, a company whose presence was a constant source of irritation to the Established Church in Great Britain. First to arrive on American soil was a young graduate of Cambridge University and minister of the Church of England with marked Puritan leanings. His name, which has come to be a symbol of religious freedom, was Roger Williams.

Boston was only five years old when he arrived. It is not surprising, therefore, that this man who possessed such conspicuous gifts and training should have been drafted at once as assistant in the Boston church. The arrangement did not last long, however, for young Williams was uncomfortable in that new "Zion in the Wilderness" which sought so persistently to regulate religious matters for everyone. He could not refrain from criticizing his fellow ministers for their evident spirit of intolerance. Quite naturally, such talk was regarded as a dangerous undermining of their earnest efforts to carve out a Christian commonwealth according to the blueprint of the Sacred Scriptures.

Accordingly it was not long before he found it expedient to move to Salem, then to Plymouth, and finally back again to Salem, where he became teacher of the church. Because he was, as it were, one born before his time, he could not be content to remain silent when the magistrates sought to regulate a man's religious worship and practice. He had absorbed in England enough of independency and Anabaptist principles to accept for himself the proposition that since vital religion is a matter of personal experience with God, each individual ought to enjoy religious liberty, and church and state ought to be regarded as distinct spheres.

The story of Roger Williams' banishment from the Massachusetts Bay Colony in 1635 is well known. Indeed, his name is lastingly associated with the great work of his life, the founding of Rhode Island Colony in 1638, with its famous guarantee of religious liberty. That he was identified with the Baptist cause for but a few months (having established what is today the First Baptist Church of Providence in March, 1639), does not lessen his importance as a consistent and courageous defender of the principle of religious freedom to which Baptists are devoted.

In our story concerning the early ministry of Baptists in America, Williams is typical of those first leaders. Educated in England, endowed with a rich cultural background, and established in the sound traditions of a developing English democracy, he brought with him that combination of steadiness, training, and daring which was so essential to the planting of the Baptist witness in the colonies.

Another who illustrates this type, perhaps even better than Williams, was John Clarke, his able lieutenant in the founding of Rhode Island Colony. A native of Suffolk in England, he had been trained abroad in medicine, possibly in Holland. He practiced in London for a time. His abilities were outstanding in several spheres of activity, including law and theology. Seeking freedom of religion, he came to New England. But disturbed by the Puritan intolerance which he found upon landing in Boston, he soon associated himself with Williams, established a Baptist church in Newport, and was largely instrumental in obtaining in 1663 the charter for the Rhode Island Colony.

Another early Baptist minister was John Myles who came to Massachusetts in 1662 when the English Parliament was imposing acts of uniformity upon dissenters. Myles was a founder of Baptist churches in Wales as early as 1649. Until he fled as a refugee, he was pastor of the Baptist church in Swansea. He brought its records and several of its members with him to America and established a Baptist church at Rehoboth in 1663. Four years later, it was moved to Swansea (Massachusetts) where he continued as pastor until his death in 1683.

Perhaps one of the most interesting leaders of the young and struggling churches in the eighteenth century was Morgan Edwards. Born in Wales in 1722, he was trained for the ministry in the Baptist seminary at Bristol, England. Then, for seven years, he served a congregation in Boston, Lincolnshire, whence he moved to Cork, Ireland, where he was ordained on June 1, 1757. After a pastorate of nine years, he returned to England to preach at Rye in Sussex. He had been at Rye not quite a year when he received, through Dr. John Gill of London, an invitation to preach in the First Baptist Church of Philadelphia. The American congregation may have sought a recommendation from the noted London clergyman who was well known on both sides of the Atlantic. At any rate, Morgan Edwards arrived in Philadelphia on May 23, 1761, and shortly thereafter became pastor of the church. In 1770 he resigned voluntarily when he observed that the work was declining. Purchasing a plantation in Newark, Newcastle County, Delaware, in 1772, he settled there and served various pastorless churches from time to time until the American Revolution.

Because of his outspoken Tory views, Edwards was virtually "silenced" by the Philadelphia Association. His position was made more difficult because at that time one of his sons was an officer in the British Army. In these later years he became addicted to the use of intoxicating beverages, the result perhaps of his unhappy circumstances. For this reason he refused, even after the war, to resume his ministerial office, although he lectured in Philadelphia and other parts of Pennsylvania and pursued the writing of his famous *Materials Towards a History of the American Baptists* (1770-1792). He died on January 28, 1795, at seventy-three years of age.[1]

Edwards played an important part in American Baptist history. Having received a sound education himself, he realized the importance of a trained ministry, and was largely responsible for arousing the Philadelphia Baptist Association to establish Rhode Island College in 1763. In addition, he had the foresight to urge that a national body of Baptists be·incorporated with the Philadelphia Association as its nucleus and head.[2]

---

[1] Based largely upon the biographical sketch provided by Dr. William Rogers, of Philadelphia, in a sermon preached at Morgan Edwards' funeral. See J. Davis, *History of the Welsh Baptists* (Pittsburgh, 1835), pp. 77-78.

[2] Morgan Edwards, *Materials Towards a History of Baptists*, I, 128.

Although his plan was rejected at the time, the principle has since been adopted, to the strengthening of Baptist work.

But not all of the Baptist ministers had come from abroad, bringing with them the benefits of Old-World training. Some were laymen who had been pressed into service and eventually had been ordained because they gave evidence of possessing special gifts. Such was William Screven, a prosperous merchant who, after arrival from England, lived first in Massachusetts, then in Kittery, Maine, where he purchased land in 1673. In 1674 he further advanced his standing by marrying Bridget Cutts, daughter of a prominent Kittery planter, who died shortly after the wedding. His mother-in-law, Mary Hole Cutts, later married Captain Francis Champernowne, nephew of the first wife of Sir Ferdinando Gorges. Screven and his wife and Humphrey Churchwood, who later married Mary Cutts, his wife's sister, were baptized in the Baptist church at Boston, Massachusetts, on July 21, 1681. His presence in Kittery must have had a salutary influence upon several of his neighbors, for a number of them were baptized during the same year.[3]

Desirous of the services of a Baptist minister, the Kittery Baptists selected William Screven and sent him to Boston with a request that the Baptist church there license him. No sooner was this done on January 11, 1682, than the magistrate and Congregational minister at Kittery began to threaten the Baptists there with fines and other penalties. When Screven himself returned to Kittery, he was summoned before the court on March 13 and accused of offensive speeches "tending to blasphemy," presumably on the subject of baptism. Rather than provide bond of one hundred pounds for his appearance at the next Court of Pleas, Screven went to jail. On April 12 his case was heard at York, and he was fined ten pounds and forbidden to hold religious services in his home or elsewhere; moreover, he was ordered to attend public worship according to the law. He paid four pounds of the fine, the rest being carried on the books. But that was the extent of his observance of the court's ruling. He was instrumental in organizing the

[3] Isaac Backus, *A History of New England with Particular Reference to the Denomination of Christians Called Baptists* (Newton, Mass., 1871), I, 400.

Baptists of Kittery into a church in 1682 and conducted meetings for them for nearly a year. These actions resulted in his being ordered by the court on October 9, 1683, to leave the province.

His movements beyond that year are a matter of some dispute. Some say that he went at once as an exile to South Carolina, where he purchased an estate near Charleston and preached. Others say that he did not actually leave Maine permanently until 1696.[4]

Still another example of a layman who eventually found his way into the ministry is Obadiah Holmes. When he came from England he united with the Congregational church in Salem. After six or seven years there, he was dismissed in 1645 to the Congregational church at Seaconck (Rehoboth). Four years later, he and a handful of others became dissatisfied because of an unrighteous act of the minister and withdrew. Possibly under the influence of Clarke at Newport, they acknowledged themselves to be Baptists and united with his church. How Holmes endured a severe public whipping for proclaiming his Baptist views at Lynn, Massachusetts, in 1651, is well known. He was a fitting successor to Dr. Clarke at Newport from 1676 until his death in 1682.

Clergymen from the Congregational ministry in New England who were converted to Baptist views during the Great Awakening constituted a third source of the Baptist ministry in the colonial period. It was not unusual for entire Congregational churches and their ministers to separate from the Established Church and its Half-Way Covenant.[5] Under the influence of preaching on personal religion and conversion, it was an easy step for Separate or New Light Congregationalists, as the revivalists were called, to safeguard a regenerate church membership by accepting believer's baptism.

The most notable of such converts was Isaac Backus, a young lad of Connecticut whose parents were pious members of the Congregational church. He relates that he was converted quietly when alone in a field on an August day in 1741. He

[4] See discussion on this point in Robert G. Torbet, *A History of the Baptists* (Philadelphia, 1950), pp. 224-26.

[5] Philip S. Evans, *History of Connecticut Baptist State Convention*, 1823-1907 (Hartford, 1909), pp. 10-11.

then was about seventeen years of age. Five years later, under the influence of a revivalist preacher at Titicut, on the river between Bridgewater and Middleborough, he felt a call to the ministry. He enjoyed fellowship with the company of New Light or Separate Congregationalists there until 1749, when the question of baptism became the subject of debate. After a severe period of wrestling with the problem, Backus became convinced that the Scriptures justify only believer's baptism. Therefore, on August 22, 1751, he was baptized.

In the meantime, conferences were being held between Separate Congregational churches and Baptists concerning the practice of intercommunion. Because they had much in common and shared the evangelistic zeal of the Awakening, both desired union. Baptist churches earnestly "gave full trial to the experiment of 'mixed communion' " (what we call today "open membership").[6] It failed, however. One after another of the churches abandoned the plan, because they recognized their inconsistency in first renouncing infant baptism and sprinkling and then affirming it afterwards by admitting into membership persons holding such views. A close communion Baptist church, constituted at Middleborough on January 16, 1756, called Backus as its pastor in the July following.

Isaac Backus was no ordinary man. He had become a Baptist minister after deep soul-searching. On several occasions he paid the price of his convictions when he challenged the right of the civil government to tax non-Congregationalists in support of the establishment. He gave hearty support to the Warren Association (of Warren, Rhode Island), formed in 1767 for the purpose of strengthening New England Baptists in their fight for religious liberty. Later he served as agent of the Association to promote the cause of religious freedom. His lengthy history of the Baptists of New England is testimony enough of his devotion to the young denomination and its principles. Ever vigorous in his evangelistic work, he preached 2,412 sermons between 1756 and 1767, and traveled almost fifteen thousand miles outside of his own parish in New England.

---

[6] Backus, *op. cit.*, II, 115. For a fuller account of Backus' conversion and entrance into the Baptist ministry, see pp. 81-88.

Isaac Backus' view of the ministry was typical of that held by most Baptists of that early day. At a time when the Congregational state church was making educational qualifications the primary requirement for ordination and standing in the ministry, he insisted that true ministers of the gospel are called into that work by the special influence of the Holy Spirit. By this, however, he did not mean to deny the need for external ordination. On the contrary, he felt that one must have a visible standing in the visible church.

A fourth source of Baptist ministers in those early days was to be found in the schools established with the aid of the Philadelphia Baptist Association and the College of New Jersey, a Presbyterian school at Princeton (now Princeton University). As early as 1722 the Philadelphia Association was seeking recruits for the ministry, young men who might be sent to school at the expense of Thomas Hollis, a London merchant who was a liberal contributor to educational causes. He had already given generously to Harvard College. Within the Association were ministers who gave leadership in education: Ebenezer Kinnersley, of Philadelphia, who in 1753 became principal of the Academy associated with the College of Philadelphia (now the University of Pennsylvania); and Isaac Eaton, who in 1756 established an academy or Latin grammar school at Hopewell, New Jersey, where he was pastor. The Philadelphia Association encouraged its member churches to support Eaton's school financially and gave it general oversight.

The Hopewell Academy prepared a number of youth who became outstanding leaders for the denomination, among whom was James Manning. Born in 1738, Manning was one of seven children of a prosperous and intelligent farmer who owned a plantation near Elizabethtown, New Jersey. He enjoyed more advantages than most boys of his time. When eighteen years of age, he left home to receive instruction at Hopewell Academy. Little did Eaton realize the destiny of this youth, his first pupil.

Soon after the completion of his studies at the Academy, Manning returned home to make a public profession of his faith and to be baptized by the pastor of the Scotch Plains Baptist Church, the Rev. Benjamin Miller, who himself was a convert of Gilbert Tennent's ministry. At the age of twenty, Manning enrolled in the College of New Jersey, from which he was graduated in September, 1762, with second highest honors in his class. In the spring of the following year, he was married, and then ordained by the Scotch Plains Church.

In July, 1763, he was delegated by the Philadelphia Association, which was greatly concerned to establish a Baptist college for the training of its ministers, to present this proposal to a company of New England Baptists at Newport, Rhode Island. With the assistance of Morgan Edwards and Samuel Jones, a graduate of Hopewell Academy, Manning secured a charter in February, 1764, from the General Assembly of Rhode Island. Thereupon, he moved to Warren, a town about ten miles from Providence, where he established an academy or Latin school to prepare students for the college, and where he became pastor of a newly organized church. In 1765 he was elected president of the college.

The new institution and its young president became a nucleus of Baptist activities in New England; for in 1767, largely under Manning's guidance, the Warren Association was organized. He conceived this plan of uniting the Baptist churches of New England for several reasons: "to promote their harmony and growth, to resist more successfully acts of oppression on the part of the 'Standing Order' in Massachusetts and Connecticut, and especially to disarm his brethren of all existing prejudices against human learning."[7] He was successful in his objectives, for the Association gave much needed support to the young school and thereby strengthened the leadership of Baptists not only in New England but throughout the country at a critical time in their history. By 1771 the college was removed to Providence, where a building had been erected.

It is perhaps not too much to say that these efforts to prepare a trained ministry combined with the cause of religious liberty to develop the first signs of a denominational consciousness among American Baptists. In 1774, for example, the Philadelphia Association joined with the Charleston (South Carolina) and Warren Associations in adopting a plan by

[7] Reuben A. Guild, *Early History of Brown University including the Life, Times, and Correspondence of President Manning, 1756-1791* (Providence, 1897), p. 72.

which every Baptist was requested to contribute sixpence annually for three successive years to the support of the college.[8] It was a significant move, for it undergirded the program with a popular support that broadened the base of denominational interest.

The college and its president were symbolic of the devotion of Baptists to the cause of religious liberty and the American War of Independence. For although the charter of the school placed chief control in the hands of Baptists, it permitted men of other denominations to serve as trustees and teachers and barred no worthy student on sectarian grounds. President Manning made a notable contribution to his country in 1786 in the Continental Congress as representative from Rhode Island. Later he worked in behalf of Rhode Island's ratification, in 1790, of the new federal constitution.[9]

The Great Awakening was instrumental in setting the standards for the Baptist ministry in America. For, as we have seen, it swelled the thin ranks of Baptist membership and brought into the fellowship many former Congregationalists who came to be known as "New Light" or "Separate" Baptists. Between 1740 and 1776 the number of churches increased from approximately sixty to 472, a tenfold gain.[10] So long as the leaders of the Baptist "New Lights" were of Congregational background with appreciation of a trained ministry, they co-operated with the Regular Baptists (as those Calvinist Baptists of the pre-revival period were called) to strengthen education. It was chiefly the Regular Baptists—primarily of the Philadelphia, Warren, and Charleston Associations—who stimulated this emphasis and jointly gave material support to Rhode Island College. To illustrate the point, we need only to recall the leadership of Morgan Edwards, James Manning, and Richard Furman in persuading the Charleston Association to set up in 1789 an education fund to train ministers.

As the revivals spread, the number of Separate Baptists increased rapidly, particularly in the South. This was due, to an appreciable extent, to the zeal of Shubael Stearns, Daniel

---

[8] *Philadelphia Baptist Association Minutes: 1707-1807*, pp. 109, 135.

[9] Guild, *op. cit.*, pp. 464-81.

[10] Frederick L. Weis, *The Colonial Churches and the Colonial Clergy of the Middle and Southern Colonies, 1607-1776* (Lancaster, Mass., 1938) p. 18.

Marshall, and Colonel Samuel Harriss of Virginia. Stearns was a former New Light Congregationalist of Massachusetts who became a Baptist in 1751. Marshall was his brother-in-law, a native of Connecticut and a Presbyterian missionary to the Mohawk-Indians between 1753 and 1754. He became a Baptist in 1754, at the age of forty-eight, while in Winchester, Virginia.

Stearns led a group of Separate Baptists from Massachusetts into Virginia to escape religious persecution, only to face restrictions and harassing there also. He established the Sandy Creek Church in what is today Randolph County. It became the mother of forty-two churches founded over a period of seventeen years. Under his guiding hand, the Sandy Creek Association was organized in 1758. For twelve years it was the center of Separate Baptists in Virginia and the Carolinas.

Marshall, an untiring evangelist, preached throughout North Carolina and Virginia between 1755 and 1760, and baptized hundreds of converts. Then, at the age of fifty-five, he went to South Carolina where he labored for ten years. He devoted the last years of his ministry to Georgia, where he preached until his death in 1784, in his seventy-eighth year. Because he was sympathetic to the patriot cause during the Revolution, he won many friends for Baptists, a fact which bore rich fruit in later years.

As wave upon wave of revivals brought an ever-increasing number of converts in the South from people of limited economic and cultural resources, the appreciation of a trained ministry became harder to find. Indeed, the Baptist churches which dotted the countryside in the face of severe persecution were limited to an untrained ministry at best—chiefly farmer-preachers with great zeal but little learning. This fact, combined with the concern of Separate Baptists to allow great freedom for the leading of the individual by the Holy Spirit, discouraged all but the simplest kind of preparation.

At first the Regular and Separate Baptists remained apart, owing to their different emphases. But their common struggle for the establishment of religious liberty drew them together. A union was effected in the eastern part of North Carolina by 1777, and in the western part, after the close of the war. In

Virginia, by 1787, the two groups were joined in a single body of United Baptists.

On the frontier the typical Baptist preacher was, as we have seen, a farmer who belonged to the people to whom he ministered. In keeping with a basic concept held by many Baptists that there should be no encouragement given to a minister to think of himself as different from a layman, they discouraged payment to him for religious services rendered. What is more, they esteemed the more highly the minister who supported himself by farming his land five or six days a week. Such a minister would preach on Sunday and sometimes hold weekday meetings. Usually, he had little or no training beyond the rudiments of reading and writing. Not only was it difficult to obtain an education, but also there was a deep-seated prejudice against an educated and salaried ministry. In Virginia, for example, early Baptists had observed that a university education was the only recommendation of many worldly Episcopalian clergymen for whose salaries they were taxed. Finally, their concept of the church as a priesthood of believers prompted them to avoid any practice that would create a "class" of ministers.

Here and there, however, there were frontier preachers who received some support. The South Elkhorn Church in 1798 raised a subscription for their minister. It consisted of "salt, corn, wheat, pork, flour, sugar, tallow and whiskey and four cash subscriptions."[11] This was the exception rather than the rule. Yet one should remember that congregations which refused to pay a salary often would generously contribute assistance to the preacher in planting or harvesting his crop, or in times of illness in his family.

The process of licensing and ordaining a preacher was familiarly known on the frontier as "raising up a brother." When an individual felt impressed that God had called him to preach, he announced the fact to the church. After a trial sermon, the congregation would either approve or disapprove of his "gifts." Approval resulted in his being given a license to preach within the bounds of the local church. Later, if he

[11] This account of the frontier preacher is based largely upon primary source materials in William W. Sweet, *Religion on the American Frontier: The Baptists* (Chicago, 1931), chap. 3. For the quotation, see p. 37.

demonstrated sufficient ability, he was permitted to preach anywhere within the bounds of the association. However, if he did not show improvement in the exercise of his "gifts," he was counseled to discontinue his efforts at preaching.

Occasionally a young man of modesty but great gifts, like John Mason Peck, would be approached by members of the church with the question, "Don't you think you should preach the gospel?" After he had disclosed his feelings on the matter, the church would vote that he should "improve his gifts" within its limits until they knew better his qualifications.

Jacob Bower was less modest and undoubtedly very nervous about the whole matter. In his *Autobiography,* he tells how, after a long struggle to respond to God's call, he jumped up on a bench at the close of the service one morning without invitation and announced that there would be preaching the following Sunday at Brother Wellborn's. Then he made for the door. When several persons stopped him to ask who was to preach, he merely replied, "Come and see."

The practice of licensing a preacher was much like that used among the Methodists with "local" or "lay" preachers. It only gave the man the privilege of preaching. Ordination, on the other hand, extended the right to administer the ordinances of baptism and the Lord's Supper and to perform weddings.

Jacob Bower has described how he proceeded from being "licensed" to being "ordained." He relates that after a hard day's work on the farm, he would read at night by a wood fire. The only books that he possessed were his English Bible, a German Testament, and a small hymnbook. For over two years (1814-16) he studied at night and preached on Sunday. When the Hazel Creek Church felt that he had improved his gifts sufficiently, they gave him in October, 1816, a written license "to preach the gospel, wheresoever God in his providence 'mite' direct." In October, 1818, having moved to Logan County, about fifteen miles away, he united with the church there and was promptly extended a call to be ordained as its pastor.[12] It was customary in those days to limit ordination to a specific pastorate.

One further example may illustrate the character of the

[12] *Ibid.,* pp. 202-03.

farmer-preachers of the early frontier. In 1820 Luke Williams, a Missouri Baptist, was licensed to preach by the Concord Church in the Mount Pleasant Association. With no available money to buy a farm, yet eager to settle his family and begin his ministry, he took over a quarter section of land which he thought he could hold for a limited period by pre-emption. He built a cabin, planted a vegetable patch and a cornfield. As soon as he had cultivated the corn with the help of his wife and little children, he left home on a preaching tour. Without assistance from any missionary society or even from the churches which he revived, he visited destitute churches in the settlements on the extreme western frontiers. Four years later he died, leaving his wife and children without a shelter they could call their own. John Mason Peck, in relating this story, protested against the strong prejudice of Baptists in those early settlements against a salaried ministry:

They made the egregious blunder that because the gospel was "without money and without price," therefore they might take the *time and the talents* of a minister of Christ for their own use, and rob him of the means of support due to his family.[18]

From such widely varied beginnings came the Baptist ministry in early America: from Great Britain, from the ranks of Congregationalists in New England, from Baptist churches and schools in the colonies, and from the plow on many a frontier farm. The most significant leadership came, to be sure, from the more settled areas of the country and from a trained ministry, such as was represented by Morgan Edwards, James Manning, Samuel Jones, John Gano, Hezekiah Smith, Isaac Backus, and Richard Furman. But undergirding that leadership were scores of heroic and self-sacrificing men, like Shubael Stearns, Daniel Marshall, Jacob Bower, and Luke Williams, whose untiring zeal resulted in the planting of churches as rapidly as the frontier unfolded westward. And varied as the ministry of Baptists was in those early days, there emerged along the seaboard, at least, and in the minds and hearts of noble souls like Luther Rice, Richard Furman, and John Mason Peck, the concept of the ministry as a calling reinforced by

[18] Rufus Babcock, *Memoir of John Mason Peck, D.D.* (Philadelphia, 1864), p. 140.

adequate training for effective service. This was to become, in later years, the basis for the larger view of the ministry that prevails today.

QUESTIONS FOR DISCUSSION

1. Why were the early Baptist ministers in the American colonies a disturbing element? Were they justified in their point of view?

2. List the four sources from which Baptists received ministers in the American colonies. Which source provided the best leadership?

3. What were the essential differences in colonial days between so-called "Regular" Baptists and "New Light or Separate" Baptists?

PROJECT SUGGESTIONS

1. In your *Notebook of Facts,* identify the following persons: Roger Williams, Morgan Edwards, William Screven, Obadiah Holmes, Isaac Backus, Shubael Stearns, John Mason Peck, Jacob Bower.

2. Read the chapter in the Supplement entitled "Isaac Backus: Spokesman for Freedom," and make a list of the characteristics which made him an outstanding minister. This list may be placed in your *Notebook of Facts.*

CHAPTER III

The Vision of a Trained Ministry

THE VISION of a trained ministry has ever been present in the minds of greathearted men, for they have been impressed by the importance of able leadership in the spread of the gospel. Among such exponents of theological education was Dr. William Staughton, founder of the first Baptist theological school in America.[1] His influence upon his own times and upon future developments in Baptist missionary and educational enterprises has been sufficiently great to justify devoting some attention to his life and accomplishments.

Staughton was born in Coventry, England, on January 4, 1770. His home was of a deeply religious character, and his precocious nature, which lent itself to poetic expressions even in childhood, was given encouragement by his proud father. When William was about seventeen years of age, his father, contrary to his son's wishes, published some of the boy's efforts in a book entitled *Juvenile Poems*. It was in this period of his development that he became a Christian and united with the Cannon Street Baptist Church in Birmingham where the Rev. Samuel Pearce was pastor. Undoubtedly this association with Pearce, who was one of the organizers of the Baptist Missionary Society, stimulated Staughton's interest in foreign missions. This interest grew in intensity in later years, and after he came to America it was nurtured by the lively correspondence he carried on with the English Baptists.

When the Rev. Richard Furman of Charleston, South Carolina, wrote in 1793 to Dr. John Rippon, famed Baptist leader in London, seeking a volunteer to come to America, Staughton was recommended. In the fall of that year, therefore, he arrived in Charleston and took up duties in Georgetown, South Carolina, where he preached for a year and a half and organized a

[1] The following account is drawn largely from Edward C. Starr, "William Staughton," *The Chronicle*, XII, No. 4 (Oct. 1949).

church. It is not clear whether the climate or the practice of slaveholding in the South prompted Staughton to move North. At any rate, he settled in New York city in June, 1795. While there he seems to have come into contact, almost at once, with Baptist leaders who were seeking to promote the cause of education. Within a short time, he became head of an academy at Bordentown, New Jersey. Late in 1798, he removed to Burlington, New Jersey, to assume management of a larger academy. When he was twenty-eight, Princeton, in recognition of his preparation of students for college, honored him with the Doctor of Divinity degree.

Although Staughton was sought by Baptists in the West and actually made a tour of Ohio in 1804, he decided to remain in the East, and so accepted leadership of the First Baptist Church in Philadelphia the next year. It was a poor and struggling congregation, but remarkable growth took place under his guidance. Ever the teacher as well as the preacher, Staughton taught in two fashionable girls' schools in the city. This was in addition to preaching four times on Sunday and carrying on a heavy correspondence and program of writing. He published a one-volume edition of John Gill's great work on doctrine, which was a classic among Baptists in England. In 1811 he prepared a history of the Baptist Mission in India, and in 1813 he issued an edition of Rippon's Hymnal, a volume of the works of Virgil, and an edition of a Greek grammar.

His leadership was equally important in the formation of the Triennial Baptist Convention (the foreign mission agency of the growing denomination) and in the preparation of a trained ministry. When the Baptist Education Society of the Middle States was organized in 1812 to assist pious young men who desired to prepare for the ministry, Staughton was appointed its tutor to provide such training. This was done in his home while he carried on his pastoral duties. The young denomination soon took note of his talents in this direction; and the Triennial Convention, influenced largely by the vision of its president, Dr. Furman, who had been responsible for Staughton's coming to America, decided in 1818 to establish an "Institution to promote Education." Staughton was at once appointed principal, and the Rev. Ira Chase of New England, his associate.

The school was conducted in Philadelphia, in a house rented for the purpose. By 1821 the number of students had increased to more than twenty. The enterprise faced the problem of financial support in a denomination which was not accustomed to place a premium on education. Of the seven collecting agents who had been appointed by the Convention, Luther Rice alone pled and begged for funds to maintain the students being taught by Staughton and Chase.

Undaunted by the almost insurmountable difficulties, the Triennial Convention, prompted chiefly by Furman, Rice, and Staughton, brought to fruition plans for the founding of Columbian College in Washington, D. C. It was intended to be the national center for the training of the Baptist leaders called for by the growing foreign and home missionary work. The theological school in Philadelphia was transferred to Washington in December, 1821, to become a department of the college; and Dr. Staughton was appointed president of the new institution. In his inaugural address he pointed out the advantages of a broad education for the responsibilities of citizenship and, in particular, for the Christian ministry. The importance which he attached to this latter objective may be seen in the following statement from his address:

In the present age, when missionaries are passing into almost every region of the earth, it is evident that, to enable them with greater facility to acquire new languages, and to translate the Scriptures from the original text, a sound and extensive education is not only desirable but necessary. . . .

He pointed out that many ministers of his day, although men with little advantage of education, were "among the most liberal encouragers of theological schools." [2]

It is worthy of special note that the cause of theological education was related closely to the missionary enterprise which had brought the Baptists of America into an organizational unity and spirit of co-operation. Both Staughton and Rice were most ardent promoters of foreign missions. The former's correspondence with the leaders of the English Baptist Mission in India was voluminous, and it was published regularly in the denominational papers of that time. Luther Rice, ever since

[2] *Ibid.*, p. 176.

his return to America from Burma in 1813, had persistently visited the churches throughout the country in the interest of the Burma Mission where his friend and colaborer, Adoniram Judson, was engaged. Like William Carey of England, both Staughton and Rice realized that the ultimate success of foreign missions was dependent upon a trained leadership on the field and at home. Again and again, Rice reminded his contemporaries that the future of foreign missions was dependent upon the vital support of strong churches at home, and the secret of strength at home, in turn, was dependent upon a prepared ministry.

The founding of Columbian College was the embodiment of Rice's vision. But this attempt to establish a national Baptist college was premature, for although the number of students seeking training increased, the required financial support did not grow proportionately. Rice and Staughton spent their strength with abandon in fund raising, but they were only two; what could they hope to accomplish among the scattered and often indifferent Baptist constituency? Baptists were more interested in the projects within their own states than in this national venture. Then, too, the majority of Baptists found the challenge of evangelism and foreign missions far more impelling than the less dramatic appeal for educational support of the entire program. Yet it must not be supposed that the enterprise was entirely futile. Quite the contrary. Although the Columbian College experiment failed and the Convention gave up the project in 1826, due to the mounting financial difficulties and the fact that many Baptists felt that the Convention should restrict itself to its original task as a foreign mission agency, it nevertheless had provided an impulse to Baptist education in America which was felt widely. This was particularly true in the older states along the eastern seaboard. There the Baptist state education societies, springing up in the early years of the nineteenth century, were endeavoring to overcome the opposition to a prepared ministry and were encouraging support for the existing schools and actively at work for the organization of still others.

Perhaps the most spectacular result of the venture was the transfer, in 1825, of the theological department of the college to

Massachusetts. At that time, Dr. Francis Wayland, who was soon to become president of Brown University, was the able pastor of the First Baptist Church in Boston. He had been influential in securing the separation of Columbian College from the Convention, because he regarded the project as a major reason for the decline in contributions to the foreign mission enterprise. Without rancor, he made it plain that in his judgment Luther Rice had divided his efforts too unequally between education and missions, and that at a time when the young mission needed a full-time director.[3]

The Boston church, under Wayland's leadership, had been active in the organization of the Massachusetts Baptist Convention in November, 1824. In fact, Wayland had become its first secretary. Then in May, 1825, a group of ministers and laymen met in the vestry of his church to organize a board of trustees for a new theological institution to be located at Newton Centre, near Boston. Wayland became the first secretary of the board. The plan at first had been to combine the theological departments of the recently founded schools at Hamilton, N. Y., Waterville, Me., and Washington, D. C. This hope was not realized.

The new institution opened on November 28, 1825; and, in view of the decision of the Convention to sever ties with Columbian College, the theological department of that institution was transferred to Newton Centre, Mass., with Ira Chase as the first professor of the new faculty.[4] The founding of this school, the first theological seminary on the graduate level for the Baptists of America, was a notable achievement; for at that time the prevailing sentiment among Baptists was that God, not man, made ministers, and that schools, therefore, were more of a hindrance than a help to the working of the Holy Spirit. No doubt, the influence of Luther Rice's noble experiment at Columbian College had been felt in New England.

Another evident influence of the early venture in theological education came through Samuel Wait, a graduate of the second class taught by Dr. Staughton in Philadelphia. He became a

[3] Francis and H. L. Wayland, *Memoir of the Life and Labors of Francis Wayland.* Two volumes. (New York, 1867), I, pp. 178-80.
[4] Nathan E. Wood, *The History of the First Baptist Church of Boston* (Philadelphia, 1899), pp. 317-18.

tutor in Columbian College in 1822 and served there for four years. While in North Carolina on a trip with Dr. Staughton to collect funds for the college, he received a call from the Baptist church at Newbern. This he accepted. From that time, he devoted himself to the development of Baptist work in North Carolina. In 1830 he helped to establish the North Carolina Baptist State Convention; he founded the Baptist state paper known as the *Recorder;* and in 1832 he co-operated in the efforts of the Convention to organize the Wake Forest Manual Labor Institute for the education of ministers. He was its first principal, and when it became Wake Forest College in 1838, he served as its president until June, 1846.

The link between Staughton, Luther Rice, Richard Furman, and the later educational developments in the South was William B. Johnson of South Carolina. During Johnson's boyhood in Georgetown, he came under the influence of Dr. Staughton, of whom he said, "I could remember more of his sermons than those of any other preacher." [5] In Georgetown also he came to know Dr. Furman, who made a deep impression upon him. During the course of pastorates at Euhaw, Columbia, Savannah, and Edgefield, Johnson combined preaching with teaching in various academies. Always he was an exponent of ministerial education, because he saw the sharp contrast between the untrained ministers of the state above Columbia and those who were educated in the middle and lower sections where the influence of the Charleston Association was strong. It will be recalled that Furman had given to that body of Baptists a leadership which inspired them to support an educated, well-trained ministry.

In fact, between 1818 and 1821, Furman and Johnson worked together for the organization of the South Carolina State Baptist Convention, formed for the purpose of producing a closer co-ordination between the district associations of churches in support of the missionary enterprise of the Triennial Convention and of the program of ministerial education. When Columbian College opened in 1822, Furman and Johnson rejoiced. When Furman died in 1825, the task of furthering the cause of educa-

---

[5] Hortense Woodson, *Giant in the Land* (Nashville, 1950), p. 4. The section on Johnson is based largely on this biography.

tion in the state fell to Johnson. He, as president of the State Convention, was instrumental in the organization in 1827 of Furman Academy and Theological Institution at Edgefield, South Carolina. It was the hope of South Carolina Baptists that their brethren in Georgia would help to support the new institution. This plan had been encouraged by Jesse Mercer and W. T. Brantly, ministers in Georgia who were staunch supporters of education and who themselves had received aid as students from the Charleston Association Education Fund.

The new enterprise did not enjoy much success, however, owing to the failure of co-operation from Georgia Baptists, the lack of both local and national support for the project, and the discouraging influence of the financial straits in which Columbian College was engulfed. In addition, Baptists in the state were not agreed as to whether the institution should combine theological instruction with general classical training. Johnson favored enlarging the school into a university which would provide a college education as well as theological training for ministers. He discouraged the continuance of the manual labor aspect of the institution, which had been intended to assist poor boys through school. He argued that the Southern temperament was not suited to such a plan. He put it rather humorously when he said, "Ardor, Sir, and not perseverance, is our Southern characteristic." [6]

The trying years of dissension between the North and the South over slavery occupied much of Johnson's attention as president of the Triennial Convention from 1841 until the break in 1845, when he was elected first president of the newly organized Southern Baptist Convention. Yet he never lost his enthusiasm for the cause of a trained ministry. From 1853 to 1858 he served as chancellor of Johnson University (now Anderson College), a school for girls in Anderson, South Carolina. The climax of his efforts for ministerial education came with the establishment in 1859 of the Southern Baptist Theological Seminary at Greenville, South Carolina. He was a trustee of the new school until his death in 1862.

To Johnson's leadership, Furman University is greatly indebted. Johnson was the planner and promoter of theological

Ibid., pp. 64-65.

education for the South. And all through his life he contributed also to the training of young women.

In the West the leading spirit in behalf of education, as well as of missionary expansion, was John Mason Peck. Born on a New England farm where it was a struggle to wrest the bare necessities of life from the rocky soil, he had received only the most elementary training. Yet his ideal of the qualifications for the ministry was so high that for several years after his conversion he delayed answering the call of God to Christian service. When, at the age of twenty-two, he began his public ministry, he sought at once to improve himself by further study, first in Poughkeepsie under the direction of Principal Barnes of the Dutchess Academy, and then in Philadelphia under the tutelage of Dr. Staughton. When in 1817 he undertook his missionary appointment in the West under the Triennial Convention, an important part of his work was to establish in St. Louis a school for the instruction of white and Negro children alike. Wherever he went, he studied how the educational needs of the people on the frontier were being met. He soon observed that three-fourths of the schools were in the control of what he called "ignorant whiskey drinking Irishmen." This he opposed with all the vigor of his spirit, and he recommended, in their place, well-trained young men from New England.

By untiring efforts and ceaseless travel, Peck, in 1818, succeeded in uniting the Baptists of Missouri, Arkansas, and Illinois in the first society to be established west of the Mississippi for philanthropic or missionary purposes. So effective was it that, within three years, more than fifty good elementary schools were created in Missouri and Illinois.[7] A like enthusiasm resulted in the planting, under his direction, of one hundred Sunday schools, which by 1825 ministered to three thousand pupils. In all of these efforts, he never lost sight of the importance of a trained ministry.

In 1826 this intrepid pioneer traveled East to lay before the Massachusetts Baptist Missionary Society a master plan for the evangelizing of the West. It included a plea for the support of

---

[7] Austen K. deBlois and Lemuel Call Barnes, *John Mason Peck and One Hundred Years of Home Missions, 1817-1917* (New York, 1917), p. 34-35.

circuit preachers, the appointment of a strong minister at St. Louis (which within a few years was to be the urban center of Missouri), and the founding of a theological school in Illinois. In pleading for the third item, Peck said to the Board:

> I cannot bear that our preachers in Illinois and Missouri should continue as ignorant as some of them are. In the three states are not less than 250 Baptist preachers. A majority of them have been raised on the frontiers, with scarcely the advantages of a common school education, and not even habituated to read the word of God in early life. Every year is adding to the number of this class of preachers. . . . What should be done? Is not the path of duty plain as the noonday sun? Furnish these men with the means of such education as circumstances admit. Establish a theological school.[8]

The Board adopted his plans, and he set out to raise the funds.

By the time he returned to his home at Rock Springs, Illinois, Peck had nearly one thousand dollars in hand. He donated a section of his farm land as the site for the new school. In addition, he devoted the labor of his own hands to the construction of the building. On November 1, 1827, the institution opened under the name Rock Spring Theological and High School. Its existence was short-lived, however, owing chiefly to its isolated location and the lack of adequate financial support. In 1831, therefore, it was closed temporarily. It was not reopened until the fall of the following year, when it was relocated at Upper Alton, and called Alton College. In 1835, the school was renamed Shurtleff College in recognition of a large donation made by a Baptist layman of Boston.

The era prior to 1850 was for Baptists, as for most evangelical denominations, a period of perennial revivals resulting in enlarged congregations, new churches, and a general spirit of enthusiasm for missions. Paralleling this fervor was the quieter, yet nonetheless continuous planting of new schools: academies, colleges, and theological seminaries. By the midcentury Baptists had thirty-five educational institutions, whereas eighty-five years earlier they had had but one.

Yet it was still a period of pioneering. With the exception of a few farsighted men like James Manning, Morgan Edwards,

[8] *Ibid.*, p. 61.

Richard Furman, Luther Rice, Jonathan Going, William Johnson, and John Mason Peck, few had seen the need for coordination and conservation of effort in the task of education. The one great venture in establishing a nationally supported institution in Washington, D. C., had failed. Instead, associations, educational societies, and state conventions stimulated achievement and frequently rivalry, often at the cost of the most effective use of their resources, which were all too meager to begin with. Baptists were not yet ready for a closely knit denominationalism. They were still in a pioneering stage where church life was too unsettled to make possible a thorough coordination of effort.

Moreover, resistance to an educated ministry was strong. The prevailing spirit of the revivals was that God, in his grace, does not need man's learning. American revivalism was essentially a witnessing movement in which anyone, however humble or untutored, if called of God, became an instrument of the Spirit to exhort men to be saved. Because the Baptists were a vital part of this movement, they were used of God to win thousands to the Savior. What many failed to realize, however, was the importance of a trained ministry for the preservation of the fruits of the revivals. This was the great contribution of those whose numbers were increasing with the years—the men and women who saw that evangelism and education are inseparable essentials upon which Christ builds his church.

QUESTIONS FOR DISCUSSION

1. What connection was there between evangelism and education? What lessons does this relationship suggest to you for today?

2. What influence did the schools established by Baptists have upon the development of the denomination? Was it worth the investment made in them?

3. What were the special qualities of leadership shown by William Staughton, Luther Rice, William B. Johnson, Richard Furman, and John Mason Peck? In what ways were they outstanding ministers?

PROJECT SUGGESTIONS

1. Place in your *Notebook of Facts* a brief description to identify the following names: Columbian College, Shurtleff College, Furman University, Francis Wayland, the Triennial Convention.

2. After reading the chapter in the Supplement entitled "John Mason Peck: Builder of Men and Institutions," make a list of the ways by which Peck got laymen to help in the cause of supporting a Christian ministry.

CHAPTER IV

The Emergence of a Settled Ministry

EXCEPT ALONG the eastern seaboard, Baptist church life in America was still in the unsettled state of pioneer home missions. Indeed, the nation itself before 1850 was two-thirds frontier. To be sure, the coming of the railroads to span the continent within two decades and the opening of new frontiers beyond the Rocky Mountains hastened the development of national feeling. In time it became apparent that Americans regarded the Far West as a significant segment of their country and an important element in their "manifest destiny" as a great people.

Through the American Baptist Home Mission Society, Baptists entered almost at once into their God-given responsibility to provide a ministry for the settlers who began to push in ever-increasing numbers toward the boundless resources of the immense Northwest and the Pacific Coast. By midcentury, missionaries had been sent to California. At the same time, the Society was pushing into Minnesota and expanding its work in Indiana, Wisconsin, Illinois, and Iowa. Within the next twenty years, its missionaries were to open such new fields as Kansas, Nebraska, Colorado, Dakota, Wyoming, Idaho, and the Washington Territory.

Although the growing tensions over slavery and the ultimate outbreak of war in 1861 had curtailed the work of the Society in the South, its service continued, especially in the older Southern states, even during the years of conflict. It gave assistance in the evangelization and education of the freedmen and also in the erection of church edifices for white as well as colored congregations. In fact, as late as 1870, one-third of all its missionary force was at work in the South.

While the period of missionary expansion continued throughout the second half of the century, there was developing during this period of change and maturing a more settled church life.

42

In fact, the history of the United States since the Civil War is a chronicle of the unprecedented development of a nation from the throes of disunity to a position of world power. Almost immediately following the cessation of hostilities between the North and South, the states turned to the task of building what they hoped would be a better homeland for coming generations. In the North, the wheels of industry, which had gained momentum from the impetus of war production, turned with ever-increasing speed to convert the natural wealth of the country into more railroads, new factories, bigger machines, new roads, city dwellings, country estates, and countless luxuries for a people grateful for the return of peace. In the South, the ruins of an agricultural pattern were lamented by its friends and trampled over by Northern fortune-seekers. The smoldering embers of hate never quite burned out, while Southerners sought, with the aid of Northern capital, to build an industrial life, to supplement agriculture, and to prepare the emancipated Negro for the right use of his new freedom. The West faced problems somewhat peculiar to itself, such as deflated farm prices, excessive land speculation, the hampering restrictions placed upon credit facilities by a conservative East, and the settling of a vast frontier.

In these years of adjustment several trends became evident in American life. One was industrialization, particularly in the East. Concomitant with the growth of factories was the accentuation of the extremes of poverty and wealth, as the workers became increasingly dependent upon the magnates of industry. Class struggle expressed itself in the organization of unions, in strikes, and sometimes in violence.

Industrialization was accompanied also by urbanization, a trend which had begun early in the century, producing striking effects upon American town life. Neighborhoods began to change in social character as the well-to-do moved into suburban homes, leaving their place to be occupied by the poorer classes of immigrants who were arriving in great numbers to find work in the cities. An urban sophistication and secularization characterized city life as the elite came into town only for business or pleasure. Urban areas developed a cultural life of theaters, museums, music halls, libraries, and clubs that would have surprised and shocked the eighteenth century Puritan. The trend was to enjoy what the increasing wealth was making possible; namely, the advantages of an Old-World culture in an American setting.

The effect upon religious life was felt increasingly, as city people found many interests which tended to divert their attention from the church. A continental type of Sunday, with its amusements, threatened to replace the Puritan Sabbath. Urban sophistication made it difficult for the evangelist, with his emotional revivalist technique, to produce in the city results such as were possible in rural areas. With the growing complexity of the large cities, political corruption became a byword for local politics. The gravitation of immigrants, who provided a rich source of cheap labor from southern European countries, only complicated the problem.

The churches of the major denominations were not indifferent to these changes and to the need for adjustment. Indeed, they participated in an era of reform which occupied their attention from the seventies through the nineties. The scope of their interests was broad, involving prison reforms, better institutions for the care of the insane, temperance, women's rights, sabbath observance, and the correction of political injustice. Only here and there, however, were voices raised in criticism of the economic system, which was lending itself to the amassing of great fortunes by the few and the seizure of power by enormous corporations whose conduct often was beyond the pale of the law.

The majority of Christians viewed poverty, intemperance, and labor's violent attitude toward capital as the result of personal insobriety and vindictiveness. The emphasis upon the sins of society, sins in which workers and employers alike were often caught, was a note to be sounded by American Protestantism in the twentieth century, not in the nineteenth. Yet, during the later years of the seventies and on into the nineties, Protestant leadership was awakened out of its complacency by the series of violent strikes and labor disorders which accompanied the economic depression of the times.

Against the backdrop of life in a changing and maturing America, Baptists developed, by the close of the century, a denominational standing within Protestantism that was of envious proportions. In fifty years, they had increased in membership from less than a million to nearly five million. Their outlook and sense of mission in relation to other denominations had broadened considerably. A fellowship which at one time had been torn by dissension between North and South had settled down to work within the framework of two major bodies of white Baptists and several groups of Negro Baptists. In the North, three great societies dominated Baptist affairs: the American Baptist Foreign Mission Society, the American Baptist Home Mission Society, and the American Baptist Publication Society. In the South, the Southern Baptist Convention gave oversight to those functions which in the North were undertaken by the autonomous societies.

The period following the Civil War was marked in Baptist circles by an advance in evangelism and education. The postwar expansion of industry mentioned above developed new riches, some of which found their way into the endowment funds of schools and educational societies. In addition to the twenty-three colleges established between 1850 and 1860, Baptists founded, after the war, four theological seminaries, three training schools for girls, six academies, eleven junior colleges, ten schools for Negroes, and seventeen colleges and universities. Like other Protestants, they invested generously in Christian education, seeking to raise the standards of their ministry, which like that of the Methodists and the smaller sects, had not been high.

It will be recalled that the early pattern of theological training among Baptists in America had been administered by their colleges. The first school to be devoted exclusively to postgraduate theological education was Newton Theological Institution, established in 1825. The second was Rochester Theological Seminary, founded in 1850, by the New York Baptist Union for Ministerial Education. Its beginning was discouraging, indeed. It began with but ten or twelve temporary scholarships of seventy dollars each, created for the purpose of assisting worthy students. There was but little more than three hundred dollars in the treasury for all other purposes. In their first report, the trustees announced that students could obtain board from the janitor for $1.50 a week, and that several Baptists in the city were willing to take students into their families to board through the year without expense. Such a story is indicative of the unbounded faith in God and the remarkable optimism so typical of Christians who still had the pioneer spirit in their hearts. Their confidence was rewarded, for by 1872, the seminary had endowed funds amounting to $113,750.[1]

It was in that year, 1872, that Augustus Hopkins Strong became its president, a position which he occupied with great success for forty years. Few men have exerted greater influence on a denomination than this man who combined in his lifetime the roles of preacher, theologian, educator, and interpreter of Baptist principles to at least two generations of ministers. From his twentieth birthday, August 3, 1856, when he was baptized into the fellowship of the First Baptist Church in Rochester, New York, he was devoted to the cause of Christ. With the exception of eleven years when he was pastor in Haverhill, Massachusetts, and in Cleveland, Ohio, he maintained his relationship with this church. He was an exemplary member, always faithful in attendance at all of its services and the teacher of an adult Bible class.

From the time that he entered upon the presidency of the seminary in 1872, he stressed to class after class of theological students that the local church is the focal point of all Christian work. During his entire administration, he maintained a close relationship between the seminary and the churches. He recognized in the churches the very nerve center of the progress of the kingdom of God. It was through the churches, he believed, that the denomination would be magnified. He earnestly contended that if *the churches* were made "the custodians and interpreters of Christ," one need have no fear for the *Church of Christ*.[2]

During his administration he increased the size of the faculty from seven men to fifteen. He built the library from almost nothing to 39,000 volumes with a permanent endowment fund amounting to $127,000. Through the generous contributions

---

[1] Augustus H. Strong, *Miscellanies in Two Volumes*, Vol. I, pp. 151-52.

[2] *Augustus H. Strong Memorial Number. The Rochester Theological Seminary Bulletin:* The Record (May, 1922), pp. 8, 30.

of Baptist laymen like John B. Trevor, of Yonkers, New York,
John D. Rockefeller, the oil magnate and his former parish-
ioner at Cleveland, and Eli Perry, of Albany, the invested
funds of the institution arose to nearly seven hundred thousand
dollars. It represented a worthy investment in the life of the
denomination, for in the period from 1850 to 1900, the seminary trained 1,447 men. Of its graduates, sixty-four became
presidents or professors in colleges or theological seminaries;
fifty-five went forth as foreign missionaries; thirty-four became
missionaries in the great West; twenty-nine became secretaries
or agents of educational or missionary societies; and ten became editors of religious journals.[3]

Once the pattern had been established of founding theological
seminaries independent of a college or university, others came
into existence. In 1859 the Southern Baptist Theological Seminary was organized at Greenville, South Carolina, with a faculty of four professors, of whom James P. Boyce, the guiding
spirit in its founding, was chairman. Its successful launching,
with twenty-six students, was indicative of the triumph of
denominational loyalty over state loyalties.

After an unhappy interruption due to the outbreak of war
between the North and South, the school was reopened on
October 1, 1865, with its original faculty, but with only eight
students. Gradually the student body increased and likewise
the financial needs. In 1866 the Southern Baptist Convention
subscribed over ten thousand dollars to its support. Seven
years later, with the Convention's approval, the institution was
moved to new quarters in Louisville, Kentucky. Although that
state had pledged three hundred thousand dollars towards its
support, the institution was faced with difficulties when a financial crash prevented complete fulfillment of the pledge.[4] In spite
of discouragements, however, the seminary grew with the
assistance of occasional generous donors. In time it took first
place among Southern theological schools and gave to the
Southern Baptist Convention a strength which was invaluable,
for it shaped the doctrinal and ecclesiastical viewpoint of the
ministerial leadership throughout the Southern States.

[3] Strong, *Miscellanies*, pp. 153, 167-68.
[4] *Southern Baptist Convention Proceedings* for 1866, p. 16; for 1873, pp. 17-19.

In 1868 a theological seminary was organized in Pennsylvania. It was the result of the removal of the theological department of the University of Lewisburg (now Bucknell University, a Baptist institution) to Chester. The new seminary occupied the building which had been erected prior to the Civil War by John P. Crozer for a Normal Institute. Since his son, Samuel A. Crozer, had given the property to the Baptists upon his father's death, the new seminary came to be known as the Crozer Theological Seminary for Baptists. As was the case with many other educational institutions, its existence had been made possible by the benefactions of a Christian businessman. The school became the third Baptist theological seminary to provide ministers for the churches in the northern states. In time it attracted students from border states in the South, some of whom returned to serve in the Southern Baptist Convention.

Efforts to establish a school for the training of ministers for the West Coast began as early as 1850 when a Committee on Education was appointed at the initial meeting of the San Francisco Baptist Association. The chairman was the Rev. Osgood C. Wheeler, pioneer missionary to California. Three years later, at a session of the Association, the California Baptist Education Society was organized. Its specific task was to bring into existence for the state a literary and theological institution. Plans were unhappily delayed when the State Convention was disbanded in 1856. The San Francisco Association, however, did not lose interest in the project. Finally, in February, 1864, a permanent board of trustees was organized to found an institution to be located at San Francisco with the name "The University of San Francisco." But the plan did not materialize, owing to the effects of the Civil War and the occurrence of an industrial depression in the state. The concern of California Baptists for a trained ministry finally bore fruit in the founding of California College in 1871, and then in the establishing of the Pacific Baptist Theological Seminary in 1889, both of which were merged in 1904 to form the Berkeley Baptist Divinity School.[5]

During the same period, Baptists in the Middle West were

[5] Sandford Fleming, *God's Gold; The Story of Baptist Beginnings in California, 1849-1860* (Philadelphia, 1949), chap. 15.

desirous of creating a training school for ministers. At an educational convention meeting at Beloit, Wisconsin, in 1851, the Northwestern Baptist Education Society came into existence, representing Baptists in Wisconsin, Illinois, and Minnesota. Its purpose was to provide an educational institution adequate to serve the states mentioned and perhaps Iowa and Michigan also. At a convention in 1860, meeting in Chicago, a second step was taken with the organization of a corporate body, to be known as the Baptist Theological Union for the Northwest, with authority to establish a seminary at Chicago. The desired institution finally came into being in 1867 under the name of the Baptist Union Theological Seminary. Ten years later it was removed from Chicago to Morgan Park, coming under the leadership of Dr. Thomas W. Goodspeed, pastor of the Morgan Park church. In 1876 he accepted the secretaryship of the Theological Union and the Seminary.

In 1871 there was opened at the Baptist Union Theological Seminary a Scandinavian Department under the direction of John Alexis Edgren, the pastor of the First Swedish Baptist Church of Chicago. He was virtually a one-man seminary, providing for Swedish theological students a two-year course in Bible, Swedish grammar and composition, pastoral theology, Greek New Testament, Bible geography, hermeneutics, Hebrew, and systematic theology. In time a third year was added. By 1884, it became evident that the needs of Swedish Baptists would be served best if they had their own school farther west in the heart of the Scandinavian work. It was moved, therefore, first to St. Paul, Minnesota, then to Stromsburg, Nebraska, and finally in 1888 back to Morgan Park where it remained until 1914, when it was once more moved to St. Paul. There it was consolidated with the Bethel Academy under the name, "Bethel Academy and Seminary of the Swedish Baptist General Conference." Its new president, Dr. G. Arvid Hagstrom, gave remarkable leadership to the institution for twenty-seven years. The school soon became a center of strength for the General Conference, which owned it and directed its program.[6] In pattern, therefore, there is a marked resemblance

[6] Adolf and Virgil A. Olson, *Seventy-five Years: A History of Bethel Theological Seminary* (Chicago, 1946), pp. 15-47.

between Swedish Baptists and Southern Baptists in their rela-
tions to their seminaries and in the denominational solidarity
which each group has achieved by such an arrangement.

Some generalizations may be in order at this point. First, it
may be observed that there was a close association of collegiate
and theological studies in the schools. This was particularly
noticeable in the colleges which continued to maintain departments of theology. It is significant of the thinking of some that
the Disciples of Christ felt that ministerial education should
be given in connection with colleges, not in cloistered seminaries. Thus they brought into existence a new type of institution for the training of ministers, the College of the Bible, the
first of which was established in connection with Transylvania
University in 1865.

In the second place, it has become evident that there was a
trend throughout the nineteenth century to establish theological
seminaries. The participation of Baptists in this movement is
an indication of their growing recognition of the need for an
especially trained leadership and of their view of the ministry
which now had been broadened to allow room for professional
training. In this respect also, the seminaries were reflecting
the impact of new influences at work in American higher education. For example, research was being restored, during the
nineteenth century, to its central place in the universities by
educators like Charles W. Eliot at Harvard and Daniel C. Gil-
man at Johns Hopkins University. In some measure also, the
lecture method was being replaced, or at least enriched by
methods that made greater demands upon the initiative of the
student. Electives were introduced and given wider scope as
the faculties were enlarged. New teaching techniques were
being introduced, such as seminars, the case method of Harvard
Law School, and the laboratory skills of the medical schools.[7]

To be sure, these innovations in higher education did not
greatly influence theological education generally until more
recent years, largely because of the resistance to change inherent within religious institutions. Yet there was evident in the
later years of the last century a desire among Baptist educators,

[7] William Adams Brown, *The Education of American Ministers,* Vol. I (New
York, 1934), p. 81.

like President A. H. Strong of Rochester Theological Seminary and President Alvah Hovey of Newton Theological Institution, to improve professional standards, to keep pace with missionary demands, to adapt the seminary curriculum and methods of teaching to the new university ideals, and to functionalize courses. Both institutions dropped the "English course" about 1890, thus requiring all applicants to have a full college training prior to admission to the seminary.[8]

A third generalization is that the widely distributed constituency of the Baptists led to a lack of crystallization of sentiment among them concerning an educated ministry. Although the second half of the nineteenth century had been one of denominational development and the emergence of a settled church life, the very nature of the Baptist movement precluded the formulation of a united view of the ministry. In some areas of the country, Baptists were still living under frontier conditions. Revivalism, with its premium upon exhortation and zeal, was a cherished inheritance even in the cities. The fact that the majority of Baptists were of a low-income segment of the population reflected itself in a degree of suspicion of any plea for standardization of ministerial education lest it militate against those who could not afford full training. But basic to all of these considerations was the fact that Baptists gave prime importance to a call of God as the chief requisite for a minister. Moreover, their concept of the church as a witnessing movement often reflected itself in a resistance to any recognition of the importance of academic preparation for the ministry. Having observed in the ministry of more formal churches evidences of what they considered a worldly professionalism and lack of spirituality, they developed a prejudice against any tendency to set the ministers apart from their congregations on the basis of professional training and skills.

On the other hand, there were Baptists who showed grave concern for a prepared leadership. For example, in the 1860's, a self-appointed group of a dozen laymen made a five-year study of the Baptist ministry with respect to educational qualifications. Their report, published in 1868, revealed that the Bap-

[8] Augustus H. Strong, *Miscellanies*, Vol. I, p. 161; George Rice Hovey, *Alvah Hovey* (Philadelphia, 1928), p. 199.

tists of New York and New Jersey had only one student in college for every seven hundred members in the churches. This lack of an educated constituency, which was typical of other states also, in all probability explains why Baptists who seemed so strong in starting schools were so weak in supporting them. It was doubtless due to the fact that a few leaders had seen the need of a trained leadership and an educated constituency, while the majority, suspicious of education, had not followed their leaders or supported their schools, or given their own children an education.[9]

It was in view of such a situation that Dr. Henry L. Morehouse, executive secretary of the American Baptist Home Mission Society, recommended in 1887 organization of an American Baptist Education Society to formulate and promulgate a program of education for the entire denomination. This was actually accomplished when the Home Mission Society held its annual meeting in Washington, D. C., on May 17, 1888, with 427 persons present from thirty-six states. The Rev. Frederick T. Gates, a young pastor in Minneapolis, became executive secretary of the new agency. Its executive board was composed of representatives from both the North and South. Thus the American Baptist Education Society was the last organizational link between the Baptists of the two sections of the country. It had within it the possibility of furnishing a tie between the Southern Baptists and those of the North, thereby helping to overcome the effects of the great separation of 1845. That it was not destined to play such a role was due largely to the fact that the churches did not give it adequate support. Instead, it had to depend chiefly upon the benefactions of a few farsighted men of wealth, chiefly John D. Rockefeller, whose support of education had been enlisted.

The first task of the Education Society was the establishment of the new University of Chicago to supersede the old Chicago University which, because of lack of funds, had closed the year before. Through the influence of President Strong of Rochester Theological Seminary upon his friend, John D. Rockefeller, Gates was finally able to secure a pledge of $600,000 on condi-

[9] Frank W. Padelford, "Contemporary Baptists and Education" and "The Story of Baptist Education," *Bulletin of Colgate-Rochester Divinity School,* Vol. VIII, No. 3 (March, 1936) and Vol. XI, No. 1 (Oct., 1938) respectively.

tion that Baptists raise an additional sum of $400,000. This gift was followed by even larger sums, totaling several millions. Members of the First Baptist Church of Chicago subscribed eighty thousand dollars. Two-thirds of the trustees and the president of the university were to be Baptists, thus assuring its denominational affiliation without requiring it to be narrowly sectarian.

The choice of the first president was a fortunate one: Dr. William Rainey Harper, who for several years had been professor of Hebrew and Old Testament Interpretation in the Baptist Union Theological Seminary at Morgan Park. Through his wise guidance, an illustrious faculty was gathered from all parts of the country, thereby providing competent instruction in all departments, including the postgraduate. In 1892 the seminary at Morgan Park was transferred to Chicago, where it became the divinity school of the new university.

Between its organization and 1900, the American Baptist Education Society received and paid to denominational schools and colleges over one and a third million dollars. In this way the leaders of the denomination sought to give aid to the heads of institutions who were struggling to keep their schools solvent. Forty-six institutions benefited, ten in the southern states, thirteen in the northern, eight in the western, and two in Canada. In 1894 Gates resigned to take charge of Rockefeller's benefactions. He was succeeded for a time by Morehouse. The major story of the work of this Society and its successor, the Board of Education of the Northern Baptist Convention, will be told in the next chapter. Suffice it to say here that the greater portion of the large sum of money distributed to the schools had come from Rockefeller. Although other philanthropists among Baptist laymen made substantial contributions to Baptist education, the rank and file of Baptists gave slim support to the cause.[10]

A fourth generalization which perhaps needs to be made concerning this period in the development of the Baptist ministry is that the Baptist insistence upon decentralization in polity often resulted in a lack of a centralized organization to effect

[10] Padelford, in *Bulletin of Colgate-Rochester Divinity School,* Vol. XI, No. 1, p. 16

and maintain control of the schools which served the denomination. This was particularly true in the North where there was as yet no national convention similar to the Southern Baptist Convention, which exercised close supervision and ownership over its seminaries. In general, Baptist theological institutions were organizations unto themselves.

In some cases, there was denominational representation on the governing boards, but ecclesiastical control was always avoided by preventing this from becoming dominant. For example, the Baptist Educational Society of the State of New York shared in the control of Hamilton Theological Seminary and Rochester Theological Seminary, and later of Colgate-Rochester Divinity School, which was the merger of the two, through the election of members of the governing board. The Divinity School of the University of Chicago, which perpetuated the Baptist Union Theological Seminary, at first was subject to it in the selection of all professors and instructors and general supervision of instruction, although full academic freedom was granted to it as an integral part of the University. Berkeley Baptist Divinity School, which probably is most closely related to the denomination of all the Northern seminaries, is governed by a board of trustees nominated by the ten Pacific Coast Baptist state conventions. The members of the faculty must be in agreement with the essentials of Baptist doctrine and polity.[11] But this degree of affiliation and control is a product of the twentieth century in American Baptist life, not of the nineteenth.

A final observation of trends in the period under consideration is that the primary concern of Baptist seminaries was the preparation of pastors for the churches. This is not to say that the schools failed to produce professors, editors, and administrators; for they did. It is rather to underscore the consciousness which has always marked Baptists, that their major responsibility is the preaching of the gospel. Thus, the ever-recurring theme is once more emphasized, that evangelism and education are inseparably associated in the minds of thoughtful Baptists.

[11] Mark A. May *et al.*, *The Education of American Ministers,* Vol. III, (New York, 1934), pp. 469-70.

QUESTIONS FOR DISCUSSION

1. What evidences were there between 1850 and 1900 that Baptists were developing a settled church life and ministry? Was this a good thing for the effectiveness of Baptist work?

2. Enumerate the generalizations made in the last pages of this chapter. What lessons do they suggest for Baptists today?

3. What was the purpose of the American Baptist Education Society? How did it prove of help to the schools?

PROJECT SUGGESTIONS

1. Place in your *Notebook of Facts* the school with which each of the following persons was in some way associated; Augustus H. Strong, John D. Rockefeller, John P. Crozer, Osgood C. Wheeler, Thomas Wakefield Goodspeed, G. Arvid Hagstrom, James P. Boyce.

2. Make a list of the ways in which Augustus H. Strong influenced Baptists. For this exercise, read in the Supplement the biographical sketch entitled "Augustus Hopkins Strong: God's Interpreter."

CHAPTER V

The Ministry in a New Age

THE NEW WORLD of change and breath-taking progress, of terrifying wars and dreadful tensions, was the product of forces already at work in the closing decades of the nineteenth century. The rise of immense urban centers, the growth of industry into overpowering corporations, the struggle of labor to assert itself in the conflict of economic rights, the emergence of new patterns of thought with the advent of Darwinian evolution and Spencerian "progress" all contributed to a radical change in American life.

The native optimism of Americans was fed from the spring of a Natural Theology which rejected the pessimism of the Calvinistic view of depraved humanity. God was a benevolent Father who did not interfere with the course of natural law and who was quite satisfied with an hour of formal worship at the close of a week of intensive profitmaking. The supernaturalism of traditional theology gave way to a liberalism which optimistically prophesied man's self-redemption through the process of his own historical development. Due to the influence of German scholarship, the Bible was subjected to the techniques of textual and historical criticism in order to ascertain the unfolding of man's search for God, which in turn was regarded as God's way of revealing himself through the course of human history.

With an emasculated theology but a boundless optimism, American religion prospered in an increasing number of devotees and an ever-widening organizational life and scope of activities. The total church membership grew from nearly twenty-two million in 1890, to thirty-five million in 1906, to forty-two million in 1916, to fifty-five million in 1926, to eighty-seven and a half million in 1950. The activism of American Protestantism gave the illusion of an increasingly successful influence in the life of the nation. Yet the invasion of secularization weakened appreciably its impact upon the culture of America. In the words of a noted historian, "religion became increasingly a social activity rather than a spiritual experience."[1]

The major denominations, to be sure, retained their authoritative dogma without allowing doctrine to sit too heavily upon them. The interest of the average church member was in observing the accepted formalities of religion and in doing good. In fact, the American concern for humanitarianism burst into flower in the early years of the twentieth century in what has come to be called "the socialization of Christianity." Christians, to be sure, had always shown a concern for the underprivileged of society and had administered charity through the centuries. But paramount to all secondary considerations of social welfare was the destiny of the human soul lost in sin. The differences in the so-called "social gospel" emphasis lay in the changed view of man and his needs and in the new concept of the function of the church. With the explaining away of the Devil and the ignoring of sin, the naturalistically inclined had come to interpret man as a person of latent possibilities for good who needs but the proper nurture in order to develop the good life. The task of the church, therefore, was to provide a good environment in society and to deal vigorously with the social ills which bring him misery and want.

Significantly enough, the leading exponent of Social Christianity was a Baptist minister and seminary professor, Walter Rauschenbusch. Born of German parents and educated partly in Germany and partly in America, Rauschenbusch became in 1886 the pastor of the Second Baptist Church in New York city. This young seminary graduate there found himself the leader of a poverty-stricken congregation situated on the border of "Hell's Kitchen" on the west side of the city. In the midst of poverty and hunger, he witnessed the daily struggle of factory workers to survive. He refused to acknowledge that the industrial crises which brought such misery to the masses were inevitable. He believed that they were inevitable only in an economic system which did not regard the welfare of all persons in society.

Mindful of the criticisms from many of his associates in the

[1] Henry Steele Commager, *The American Mind*. (New Haven, 1950), p. 167.

ministry, he examined the Scriptures to discover an adequate directive for his ministry. This he found in Jesus' teachings concerning the "kingdom of God," which he believed offered redemption of the social system as well as of the individual.[2] For eleven years he devoted himself to the working people of New York city, extending his influence far beyond his own parish as he lectured and worked in behalf of social and economic reforms.

He was the primary inspiration of the Brotherhood of the Kingdom, a group of ministers who organized in 1892 to study the implications for their generation of the New Testament teachings concerning the kingdom of God. Rauschenbusch continued to give leadership to this movement while he was professor at Rochester Theological Seminary from 1897 until his death in 1918. During this period he sought to undergird the social expression of Christianity with a philosophy and a theology. This he did in three great books: *Christianity and the Social Crisis* (1907), which made him famous; *Christianizing the Social Order* (1912); and *A Theology for the Social Gospel* (1917).

In his theology, Rauschenbusch did not deny the importance of the personal relationship of the believer to Jesus Christ. Always he insisted upon the importance of regeneration and personal faith. Neither did he deny the redemptive character of Christianity, as did many other exponents of the "social gospel." Rather, he shifted the central position of emphasis from the doctrine of the personal and mystical union of believers in Christ to the doctrine of the kingdom of God as the way of life for the community of believers as they live corporately in the world. From the vantage point of the midcentury, Rauschenbusch, were he living today, might recognize that in his inclination to blame social institutions rather than individuals for the evils of mankind, he had put too much faith in the concept of progress and had not given sufficient weight to the selfishness of human nature.

The ministry of Walter Rauschenbusch, although not typical of Protestant ministers, does illustrate the problems which confronted the thoughtful minister in that trying period of transi-

[2] Dores R. Sharpe, *Walter Rauschenbusch* (New York, 1942), p. 62.

tion. He was faced by a changed society. Its needs grew out of the fact that the people had been uprooted from their old associations, which had been predominantly rural or small-townish, and were trying desperately to adjust themselves to the new conditions of an urban-industrial pattern. At the same time, the minister was faced with the complexities of great combinations—economic, industrial, and financial—which controlled ever larger areas of life. He saw his government assuming to manage an increasing proportion of men's affairs. He was not unaware that this trend had deprived him, in large measure, of an important aspect of his pastoral office, namely, the dispensing of Christian charity. If he were astute, he could hardly escape the unpleasant fact that the public press had relieved him and his fellow ministers of a portion of their traditional work—the interpretation of events and the shaping of community opinions and ideals.

In the solution of these problems, he had two possible courses of action. He might refuse to assume any responsibility for giving guidance to his congregation in the economic and political questions with which they were confronted, on the ground that he, as a minister of the church, should not become involved in secular matters. Or he might include in his conception of his duties as a minister the social as well as the individual problems of his congregation, and endeavor to minister to those needs in terms of the guiding principles of the Christian gospel. If he chose the latter course, he would be compelled at once to decide what position he should take with reference to such knotty questions as might be involved in his relationship to war as a means of settling disputes, to liberal economic theories which challenged traditional *laissez-faire,* to psychiatry's varied theories concerning the basic ills of mankind, to interracial issues at home and on foreign mission fields, and to the developments in scientific thought which challenged traditional interpretations of the Bible.

Furthermore, the alert minister soon realized that he faced a changed intellectual outlook from that of his father or grandfather. The climate of opinion, especially between the two world wars, reflected a detachment of religion from its central place in education. This had resulted, of course, from the loss of a commonly accepted philosophy of life. Although the heritage, at least of old-stock Americans, was Protestant, either the failure to attend church or the indifference of Christians to the shaping of a Christian philosophy of life had left a whole generation of people in theological ignorance. Indeed, in many philosophical classrooms, not only was a simple faith in God called in question, but also the possibility of a valid philosophic basis for norms of social conduct was challenged. In education a functional view was developed, which attempted to relate the content of knowledge to its use. This trend had a dual influence upon the teaching of religion: it introduced a more vital approach to teaching techniques, but it also combined with the secular spirit of the times to determine the validity of content by a pragmatic test which did not always make allowance for the deeper spiritual needs of the individual or for an adequate Christian theology.

The effect of these complex influences upon American Protestantism was to produce a growing unrest in the churches. It was most noticeable among the Episcopalians, the Presbyterians, the Congregationalists, and the Disciples. The Baptists were affected also, but perhaps to a lesser extent because of their predominantly rural character. But in areas served by college and seminary graduates who had received training from institutions which reflected the "new learning" that sought insights from historical criticism, textual criticism, sociology, psychology, biology, and other fields of research, tensions were aroused between traditional orthodoxy and what came to be known as theological liberalism. Sometimes, however, the cause of restlessness was not theological, but was due to a confusion on the part of ministers and churches alike about their social responsibility. As leaders of the organized denominations began soon after the turn of the century to set up social-service commissions and departments of research in an effort to awaken the concern of laymen and to educate them to the needs about them, certain elements became vocal in opposition to the trend. Frequently, the charge was made that liberal social and economic views went hand in hand with liberal concepts of doctrine.

This reactionism within all of the major denominations of

Protestantism was known as fundamentalism. Its spokesmen called for a strict belief in the inerrancy of the Bible, in the deity of Jesus Christ, in the substitutionary atonement of his death, in the bodily resurrection of the Savior, and in his personal and imminent return to the earth to usher in the Millennium. They were equally ardent in opposing biblical criticism, the historical interpretation of the Bible, the theory of biological evolution, the liberal social views expressed by the Federal Council of the Churches of Christ in America (organized in 1908), and the trends in some theological seminaries to offer such courses as sociology, philosophy of religion, and counseling, which they regarded as weakening biblical and theological studies.

A further evidence of the effect of these trends upon the churches and the ministry was to be seen in the growing restlessness on the part of seminary graduates during the first two decades of the twentieth century. The net losses of seminary graduates to the ministry per year were twice as heavy for the classes of 1915-19 as for the classes of 1900-04. On the basis of a survey, it was discovered that the net loss to the ministry in 1915-19 was 13.5 per cent, while the net gains for nonreligious work was 111.7 per cent. In other words, there was an increasing tendency on the part of seminary graduates to abandon the ministry for nonreligious work.[3] Several factors were very likely responsible for this trend, among which were the uncertainty surrounding the war years and for some the loss of a vital faith and sense of mission in the face of the growing secularism of the times. The seriousness of the trend became more noticeable when it was found that in 1926, colleges and seminaries provided only 18 per cent of the new ministers required for the churches, whereas the proportion had been 30 per cent in 1874.[4] It was quite evident that during a period of phenomenal rise in the educational level of the general population, the educational level of the ministry had been falling.

It becomes clear, upon reflection, that secularization of education in the colleges and universities had cooled the ardor of many young men heading for the ministry and had diverted

[3] Mark A. May *et al., The Profession of the Ministry: Its Status and Problems.* Vol. II of *The Education of American Ministers.* (New York, 1934), p. 33.
[4] *Ibid.*

them into channels of service offering more material reward. The old-line seminaries had been influenced, to some degree, by the rationalistic trends in German theology and biblical criticism, with the result that some students in their confusion turned to types of church service other than preaching or went into nonreligious work. Dissatisfaction with these trends in Baptist theological education expressed itself in the forming of new seminaries to provide the traditional orthodox teaching of earlier days.

In 1913 the Northern Baptist Theological Seminary was founded in Chicago, largely under the guidance of the Second Baptist Church. It represented a protest against a liberal type of teaching then being offered at the Divinity School of the University of Chicago. The curriculum of the new school was adapted to the needs of those who were not academically qualified for admittance to standard seminary courses. At the same time, the Norwegian Baptist Theological Seminary came into existence, in affiliation with Northern. In 1925 a group of Conservatives, some of whom were leaders in the Fundamentalist Fellowship of the Northern Baptist Convention, established The Eastern Baptist Theological Seminary in Philadelphia. Some of its founders and early professors were alumni of Crozer Theological Seminary in nearby Chester, Pennsylvania. To ensure a preservation of its orthodox witness, its trustees and faculty were required to subscribe annually to a doctrinal statement.

Two additional seminaries, not listed in the American Baptist Convention Yearbook, are the Western Baptist Theological Seminary in Portland, Oregon (organized in 1927), and the California Baptist Theological Seminary, founded in Los Angeles, California, in 1944. As a result of the open break in 1943-47 between the Convention and the Fundamentalist element within the Convention, certain of the Fundamentalists (now called Conservatives) brought into being the Denver Conservative Baptist Theological Seminary in Denver, Colorado. Its faculty and trustees are not only required to sign a doctrinal statement annually, but also they are prohibited from any association with the American Baptist Convention.

Other Baptist schools which have come into existence since

1900 to train ministers and other Christian workers are Central Baptist Theological Seminary, Kansas City, Kansas (1901), which being located in the Middle West, serves churches of both the North and the South; the Spanish American Baptist Seminary in Los Angeles, California (1913); the Baptist Woman's Missionary Union Training School at Louisville, Kentucky (1907); Southwestern Baptist Theological Seminary, which developed out of the Department of Bible Teaching at Baylor University at Waco, Texas, and became a separate institution in 1908; New Orleans Baptist Theological Seminary at New Orleans, Louisiana (1918); and Southeastern Baptist Theological Seminary, organized in 1952 at Wake Forest, North Carolina. The last four mentioned are schools of the Southern Baptist Convention.

The establishing since 1900 of at least a dozen theological training schools, including the American Baptist Theological Seminary founded in 1924 and supported jointly by the National Baptist Convention, U.S.A., Inc. (Negro) and the Southern Baptist Convention, indicates a virility among Baptists. Altogether, Baptists in the United States have approximately twenty seminaries and three training schools for religious workers. However, when one realizes that there are nearly eighteen million Baptists in the country, it becomes obvious that these schools cannot begin to supply the need for ministers to serve at least sixty thousand congregations. One may well ask how and where the great bulk of ministers are trained; and the answer is that a large percentage are untrained, a sizable number have had only meager training (often from non-Baptist schools), and the remainder are products of Baptist seminaries, some affiliated with one convention and some with another, or are independent of any denominational association.

The process of developing co-operation and denominational direction for theological education and for the placement of ministers in the churches has made slow progress. In the previous chapter we referred to the organization in 1888 of the American Baptist Education Society to formulate and promulgate a program of education for the denomination. Soon after the Northern Baptist Convention came into existence in 1907, a group of college presidents urged the Convention to establish a permanent Board of Education. This was done at Philadelphia in 1911. It was to be composed of twenty-one members. At the next annual meeting, in Des Moines, Iowa, the American Baptist Education Society, which had become dormant since Rockefeller had withdrawn his support a few years before, was revived. Constitutional changes were made so that members of the new Board of Education should always constitute the Board of Managers of the Education Society. Professor Ernest D. Burton of the University of Chicago was chairman of the Board for twelve years. Dr. Frank W. Padelford, who was secretary of the Massachusetts Baptist Missionary Society (Massachusetts Baptist Convention), was appointed executive secretary of the Board. He held this position for twenty-nine years. The Board actually began to function in 1912, when funds were voted for its support by the Northern (now American) Baptist Convention.

The first task of the Board was to take a census of the religious affiliation of students in practically all of the colleges and universities in the North. It was found that there was but one Baptist student for every 176 church members, one Methodist for every 143 members, one Presbyterian for every 70 members, and one Congregationalist for every 69 members.[5] In the thirties, the Board discovered that of some 5,500 Baptist ministers in the North, 35 per cent had received college and seminary training, while 31 per cent had received no more than an elementary or high school education. (The 3,000 ministers who did not report their educational background may not have had much to report.) This was an unfavorable report, in comparison with Presbyterians, 69 per cent of whose ministers had had college and seminary education; with the Episcopal rectors, 61 per cent of whom were in this category; and with Congregationalist ministers, 51 per cent of whom so qualified.[6] The situation, clearly, was serious.

While the Board of Education directed much of its attention to the colleges, university pastorates, academies, and training

[5] Frank W. Padelford, "Contemporary Baptists and Education," *Colgate-Rochester Divinity School Bulletin*, Vol. VIII, No. 3, p. 201.

[6] *Ibid.*, p. 204.

schools, it did not neglect theological education. In 1942, in spite of the preoccupation of the country with a great world war and perhaps because many serious-minded people were realizing more than ever before the importance of strong churches and an able Christian leadership, the Board appointed a Committee on Recruiting for the Ministry. It was a step in the direction of attracting into Christian service able and consecrated young people—those who in the course of their education might otherwise be diverted into other callings.

Following upon the retirement of Dr. Padelford in 1941, the Board of Education was merged in 1944 with the Board of Managers of the American Baptist Publication Society. The new agency became known as the Board of Education and Publication of the Northern Baptist Convention (now the American Baptist Convention). Its administration was assigned to Dr. Luther Wesley Smith, who serves concurrently as executive secretary of the Publication Society and of the Board of Education. The chairman of the new agency was Dr. W. W. Charters, a noted educator who served in this capacity until his death in March, 1952.

Upon the recommendation of these two men, the Board of Education and Publication undertook a survey of theological training in the Convention between 1943 and 1945 under the professional direction of Dr. Hugh Hartshorne, assisted by Dr. Milton C. Froyd. It was revealed that "31.9 per cent of the ministers in Convention churches have had no college training whatever, 9.8 per cent have had no more than high school training, and 22.1 per cent have had only theological training; and that 19.1 per cent of the ministers who are in the pastorate have had no theological training of any kind, either seminary or Bible institute."[7] Of the 68.1 per cent of ministers who have had some college training (one year or more), 19.8 per cent received it in Baptist colleges, 36.1 per cent in other colleges, and 12.3 per cent in theological colleges which are departments of the newer seminaries established since 1900. Schools of this latter type were found to have made a significant contribution to the improvement in the educational preparation of min-

[7] Hugh Hartshorne and Milton C. Froyd, *Theological Education in the Northern Baptist Convention* (Philadelphia, 1945), pp. 99-100.

isters. "The number entering the ministry without college training has been cut from 38.6 per cent before 1920 to 23.2 per cent since 1935." Since 1935 "they have contributed 19.8 per cent of the college training of the entire ministry in the Baptist denomination." Because of their large enrollment, these schools have increased appreciably "the over-all output of the Baptist seminaries."[8]

While there had been an apparent gradual rise in the cultural and theological training of Baptist ministers, the total proportion of those having a standard college and seminary training has not increased appreciably beyond 36 per cent in a quarter of a century. At the same time, the number of ministers without training in *Baptist* schools was found to approximate 53 per cent, a factor which represented a serious threat to the maintenance of a strong denominational emphasis.[9]

Thoroughly aroused by the findings of the survey and determined to strengthen the leadership of the churches, the Department of Theological Education of the Board of Education and Publication (of which Dr. Froyd was director), the Committee on Ministerial Education, and the co-operating agencies of the American Baptist Convention united in sponsoring an epoch-making event. For the first time, the American Baptist churches, on a broad basis of representation, faced the problem at a Conference on Professional and Lay Leadership, held at Green Lake, Wisconsin, August 5-8, 1950. The chairman was Dr. Wilbour E. Saunders, president of Colgate-Rochester Divinity School. One hundred and thirty persons representing every state within the area of the Convention participated in the planning sessions, out of which was forged a program of advance for ministerial education in terms of nine major objectives. The great areas of concern covered by the program were in-service training for pastors, recruitment of able men and women for the ministry, strengthening of the seminaries in financial resources, lifting of ordination and placement standards for the ministry, and a raising of adequate financial support for pastors.

   [8] *Ibid.*, pp. 102-03.
   [9] Milton C. Froyd, "Are We Heading Toward Denominational Disintegration?" *Missions*, Vol. 37, No. 8 (Oct., 1946), p. 488.

The implementation of the program was entrusted to a Commission on the Ministry appointed by the General Council of the Convention at Cleveland, Ohio, in 1950. President Saunders was made its chairman. It held its first meeting on December 4, 1950. In April of the year following, Dr. Lynn Leavenworth succeeded Dr. Froyd as director of the Department of Theological Education. A further outgrowth of the planning conference of 1950 was the Conference on the Development of Lay Leadership, similar in pattern, which was held at Green Lake July 23-27, 1952.

The era of transition has been one in which American Baptists have come to realize, as never before, the importance of a trained and consecrated leadership. There have always been a few men of vision who have seen the advantage of adequate preparation for the heavy task of the ministry. But today, although some still view with a degree of fear and suspicion the lifting of educational standards, an increasing company of men and women believe that God can do more with a prepared man than with an unprepared man. Yet all Baptists are agreed that the first requisite of a good minister of Jesus Christ is the call of God to a man of holy life. One may put it in the words of Peter Marshall, who defined it as "the 'tap on the shoulder' [which] is the almighty power of God acting without help or hindrance upon an elect fallen sinner, so as to produce a new creature, and to lead him into the particular work which God has for him." [10]

QUESTIONS FOR DISCUSSION

1. Why was the period following 1880 and down to the present a "new age"? Were the forces at work helpful or a hindrance to the spread of the gospel?

2. What new demands did this "new age" make upon Baptist ministers?

3. How has the work of the American Baptist Education Society been enlarged and made more effective by the present Board of Education and Publication?

[10] Peter Marshall, *Mr. Jones, Meet the Master* (New York, 1949), p. 31.

PROJECT SUGGESTIONS

1. On an outline map of the United States which you can place in your *Notebook of Facts,* locate all of the Baptist seminaries and colleges which have been mentioned in questions of previous chapters and those named in this chapter. Circle the location of those which are associated with the American Baptist Convention.

2. After reading the chapter in the Supplement entitled "Walter Rauschenbusch: Prophet of Social Righteousness," list the ways in which this Baptist minister and seminary professor tried to meet the needs of the "new era."

CHAPTER VI

The Ministry for Tomorrow

AMERICAN BAPTISTS at the midcentury were still more than fifty per cent a rural and small-town people. Of the 7,481 churches, representing a membership of over a million and a half, fifty per cent were congregations of less than 140 members and were located in communities of a population under 2,200. To serve this number of churches, there were 5,305 ministers, sixteen per cent of whom ministered to two, three, or four congregations, each of which was unable to support a full-time pastor. They all labored under the handicap of almost subsistence income. In 1951 the average salary received by pastors in the American Baptist Convention (not including parsonage) was $3,031. This represented an increase of only thirty-nine per cent during the previous six years, while the cost of living had risen forty-four per cent in the same period.

It is understandable, therefore, that the denomination was faced with grave problems which had to be solved, if its leadership was to be strengthened to meet the increasingly complex needs of society in an era of transition. There was the necessity of lifting the standards for ordination in order to assure the churches of a better trained ministry. There was also the problem of securing a higher salary level for ministers who were severely handicapped by economic strain. In addition, there was the whole question of relationships between the Baptist ministry and that of other denominations in the interest of a general advance of evangelical Christianity in a period of wide population shift throughout the country.

Because new communities have sprung up virtually overnight, the task of planting new churches once again faces all major Protestant communions. But the rising educational level of the rank and file of Americans imposes the necessity of a leadership superior to that required in the "pioneer" days of the last century. Paramount to all of these considerations, for Baptists at least, is the importance of a restudy of the nature of the church and the ministry. And this, for the reason that Baptists, who have made their greatest contribution at this point, namely, the return to the New Testament concept of the church as a fellowship of witnessing disciples, are in grave danger of losing sight of that which is their genius.

Plagued on the one hand by a secularism which has brought a certain complacency into church life and harassed on the other hand by a "dispensational" view of the church which often has been held to justify the most flagrant schism, Baptists find themselves once again forced back to a fresh study of the New Testament. And this is as it should be. For while American Baptists are not narrowly sectarian, they need the stimulus which comes from the consciousness that their principles are worthy of preservation and propagation.

Their confusion concerning the nature of the church has not been due to the lack of a formulation of such a doctrine by their forefathers, but rather has been caused by an infiltration into Baptist pulpits and Sunday schools of a teaching that regards the organized denominations as apostate, while it insists that the separation of the remnant of true believers is the will of God. Very often the basis for separation is not a difference on basic points of theology or on the standards of holy living, but on matters of ecclesiastical association. Thus there has developed within Baptist circles an opposition from some quarters to the willingness of the American Baptist Convention to cooperate with other Protestant bodies. And from some, there has even arisen a protest against membership within the Convention itself.

Impressed by the gravity of the issues confronting them, state convention leaders throughout the American Baptist Convention began to meet in 1951 and 1952 to study the major problems in the light of the nine-point Platform of Advance adopted by the Commission on the Ministry. With the assistance of the Department of Theological Education under the direction of Dr. Lynn Leavenworth, conferences were held to give guidance as to the best course of action.

Leaders have been encouraged to make uniform the ordination procedures to be followed in their respective state conventions. Because Baptists traditionally have been fearful of minimizing the divine call as the primary requirement for entrance into the ministry, local ordaining councils in some places have been very hesitant about imposing academic requirements upon candidates for ordination. However, the present situation, which calls for a superior leadership with special training and skills, has impressed upon many the fact that such standards are necessary. Moreover, it has been demonstrated that men with equal consecration plus college and seminary training accomplish more in their churches than those who lack such preparation.[1] Another factor which has helped in making the standards for ordination more uniform is that only about thirty-eight per cent of the ministers in the American Baptist Convention, according to figures released in 1945, had graduated from *Baptist* seminaries. Thus was there evidence in the ministry of a training which was not adequate and not sufficiently Baptist.

Equally urgent has been the need for better procedures in the placement of ministers in the churches. Owing to the adherence to a congregational polity which avoids interference with the local church in its selection of a pastor, a variety of practices have arisen through the years. Young men coming out of Bible schools, colleges, or seminaries have found themselves dependent upon one of three sources of assistance: a placement office in their school, if it has one; the help of a friendly pastor who has contacts with pastorless churches; or the aid of a state convention secretary to whom some churches look for guidance in the choice of a minister.

The lack of uniformity of procedure has, in many cases, opened the door for unhappy results. In some instances, young men who knew little about Baptist polity or the relationships of a local church to its denominational program received access to a Baptist church, without counsel or supervision. If the individual had a mind to do his share in the fostering of co-operation by his congregation in the denominational program, he was not always aware of how best to proceed. And if he was not so minded, he was wide open to the influences of other groups

[1] William Adams Brown, *Ministerial Education in America,* Vol. I of *The Education of American Ministers* (New York, 1934), p. 55.

who sought from him and his congregation financial and spiritual support for their program. The result was that the denominational missionary program lost the support of a significant company of people, and the Convention fellowship was the poorer for the absence of a sister church.

Experienced ministers face some of the same problems. If a minister desires relocation, he must pursue one of several courses: consult with his friends in the ministry and hope to be recommended to another church; confide in the state secretary of the convention in which his church is situated; correspond with a neighboring state secretary in the anticipation of friendly counsel and consideration; or boldly write to a pastorless church to offer his services, a procedure which is avoided by many ministers.

The problem is equally severe for a church which is in need of a pastor. The typical pulpit committee is often the victim of confusion and lack of direction. With a fear of outside domination, some committees studiously avoid seeking counsel from the state secretary of the convention. Instead, they read hopefully the letters of application which come to hand, often before the present incumbent has left his post of service. Or they may communicate with some pastor whom they have heard desires a change and who appears to be a likely candidate. On some occasions a free-lance minister may appear in the community and seek a "hearing" before the congregation. All too frequently, his offer is accepted. If he has a forceful personality, he may convince the congregation by this single visit that he is "the man of God's choice." The call is extended and accepted, only to be regretted by the unwary church within a few short weeks or months. The fault, of course, lay with the church which did not check with denominational leaders who were in a position to give counsel about the past records of prospective pastors. Even when a pulpit committee exercises care in the selection of a candidate, it may not be in a position to secure all of the information necessary to determine the full qualifications of preparation, experience, attitudes, and character, so essential in a pastor, if he is to lead them in a happy relationship to their denomination and to the wider fellowship of Christians.

To help the churches solve such problems and to give guidance to ministerial students and pastors in respect to placement, the State Conventions and the Department of Theological Education of the Board of Education and Publication are endeavoring to work out procedures in co-operation with theological seminaries and the national Ministers' Council. The greatest hurdle to be overcome in this task is the fear in the minds of many Baptists that such assistance will deprive the local church of its freedom in the selection and call of a minister. The Board of Education maintains a National Registry of Candidates for full-time Christian leadership. It includes the names of all students preparing for any of the church vocations for which the churches or schools of the denomination need consecrated men and women.

Another area in which American Baptists are making some advance is that of what may be called "in-service training." It is a program to make available for full-time pastors further training while serving their churches. The seminaries are in the lead in the development of such projects. Andover Newton Theological Institution launched recently a four-year curriculum in order to allow one year of supervised training for students while engaged in actual church service. Colgate-Rochester Divinity School introduced in 1950 a supervised Field Work Program for which the sum of $350,000 was raised. Central Baptist Theological Seminary has developed a rural church program to answer the demands for a specially equipped ministry for rural pastorates. Linfield College in Oregon and Alderson-Broaddus College in West Virginia are co-operating with the Department of Theological Education of the Board of Education and Publication in projects which offer courses for academic credit to ministers while continuing their pastorates. Howard College in Alabama developed a few years ago a Plan of Extension Training under the leadership of Dr. Gilbert L. Guffin, now president of The Eastern Baptist Theological Seminary. It has provided a pattern for projects in other states where a college, the state convention, and the Department of Theological Education can work together to offer training to ministers who were prevented by limited resources and family responsibilities from securing an adequate education in their youth.

One of the most pressing problems facing Baptists today is the crisis in Negro ministerial education. In January, 1948, Dr. George D. Kelsey, noted Negro Baptist educator and associate executive director of the Central Department of Field Administration of the National Council of Churches, discussed this subject before a Joint Committee of the Northern (now American) Baptist Convention, the Southern Baptist Convention, and the National Baptist Convention, Inc. He pointed out that the environment of Negro Baptist church life does not encourage the most alert and capable young men to enter their ministry. The generally accepted view that theological learning is harmful to the work of the Holy Spirit, and the attitude of many candidates for the ministry that the churches are run by unlettered leaders who resent careful preparation, have combined to discourage recruitment of the best Negro youth for the ministry. As of the winter quarter of 1945, only 327 Negroes were engaged in graduate theological study in the entire country, while several times that number were pursuing short-term courses in Bible Institutes of varying types. The gravity of the situation was underscored in the following statement:

> At present the state of the Negro church and its ministry is reflected in the shift of Negro intelligentsia from Baptist and Methodist churches, in which they were reared, to Episcopalian, Congregational, Presbyterian, and Catholic churches. There is also a shift from the smaller 'common' churches to the larger, semi-sophisticated Baptist and Methodist churches, thus leaving the majority of churches to ignorant preachers and laymen. More than is generally realized, many Negroes are simply leaving their churches without making any new church attachment.[2]

Dr. Kelsey further pointed out that the urban Negro is rapidly coming under the sway of the labor leaders and the politicians, whereas once he was under the influence of his minister. Moreover, as the present trend in labor unionism provides him with more leisure-time activities, his thinking will be affected increasingly by secular rather than Christian leadership.

As a means of facing realistically some of these problems, a survey of Negro Baptist theological education within the United

[2] George D. Kelsey, "The Present Crisis in Negro Ministerial Education." In mimeographed form in possession of the writer.

States was completed in 1952 by Dr. Ira De A. Reid, professor of sociology at Haverford College in Pennsylvania. Working under the direction of the Joint Survey Commission of the Baptist Inter-Convention Committee, representing the three major Baptist conventions, Dr. Reid revealed certain interesting facts: First, that there are three types of schools for the training of Negro leadership: those affiliated with the Board of Education of the American Baptist Convention; those founded and controlled by Negro Baptist state conventions; and the American Baptist Theological Seminary at Nashville, Tennessee, which is supported jointly by the National Baptist Convention, Inc., and the Southern Baptist Convention. Second, that about 500 Negro Baptist ministers a year are needed for replacements in the churches. At present, only one-fifth of that requirement is being met. Third, at least one-half of the current ministry for some forty thousand churches has had no formal training at all of a professional character. In the territory of the Southern Baptist Convention, over ninety-one per cent of the Negro Baptist ministers have had no special training, while less than one per cent hold college degrees.[3] In its analysis of the leadership situation among the Negro churches of the South, the study parallels the Hartshorne-Froyd survey of American Baptist churches completed in 1945.

The warnings issued by Dr. Reid and Dr. Kelsey concerning the Negro ministry may be sounded also for certain aspects of the white ministry, for some of the same problems exist among white Baptists (although perhaps not so acutely) as prevail among their colored brethren.

To be a minister in this day of specialization is a much more demanding task than it was fifty years ago. The typical minister today is called upon to perform a multiplicity of tasks, any one of which calls for some special training and skill. He is expected to preach at least two sermons a week and to deliver numerous addresses on special occasions. It is his responsibility to administer the various departments of the church. Personal counseling and general pastoral care are considered a twenty-four-hours-on-call part of his job. He must show some interest

[3] Ira De A. Reid, *The Negro Baptist Ministry: An Analysis of Its Profession, Preparation and Practices.* A mimeographed report submitted to the Joint Survey Commission for study and publication.

in community organizations and devote some margin of time to committee work, if he is to make any impact upon his town. If his church is to maintain any vital relationship to its denomina-' tional program, he must find time to attend associational and state convention gatherings and committee meetings.

To underscore even further the complexities of the ministry in our day, we have but to enumerate the various types of specialized service into which ordained workers go: directors of Christian education, university pastors, hospital and prison chaplains, ministers of youth, and posts of denominational leadership.

The other side of the picture is that the average minister often thinks too narrowly of his responsibility as a minister of Jesus Christ. All too frequently he views his work only in terms of preaching, pastoring, and administering, to the exclusion of educating his people. This last responsibility, if it is to be done well, calls for a measure of specialized training.

Thus there are two dangers which the ministry of tomorrow must avoid. One is to reflect so greatly the secular trends of the times that the minister becomes a promoter and administrator of a kind of "Christian activism" that permits little or no room for the development of the spiritual leadership so desperately needed. The other danger is to fit so complacently into a narrow concept of the duties of the minister as to allow no fulfillment of the threefold commission which our Lord gave to his disciples: to preach, to administer the ordinance of baptism, and to teach.

So noble is the calling of the ministry and so heavy are the responsibilities placed upon those who respond that every assistance should be given to the men of God who undertake to fulfill the Great Commission. It is at this point that the consecrated laymen of our churches, who also have been redeemed and called to be witnesses and servants of God, although in different fields of occupation, can uphold the glory of the ministry of Jesus Christ.

This can be done in a number of ways. First, the laymen should safeguard the ministry with the finest standards of ordination and placement. Second, they should provide an adequate living for the minister whom they have engaged, so that he can devote his full time to their church and its community outreach. Third, they should give every encouragement to their minister to improve his effectiveness by allowing him opportunity for refresher courses, for purchase of books, and for attendance at conventions, conferences, and institutes conducted by his denomination. Fourth, laymen should undergird the need for a trained ministry by providing financial support to the colleges and seminaries which have been founded under God to prepare a ministry for the spread of the gospel. Fifth, laymen can meet the need of congregations which require temporary assistance in a time of stress by encouraging the development of lay preachers, who shall be trained to preach and to assist the churches until a fully trained man can be secured. Sixth, laymen can vitalize the ministry by joining hands with the minister in a seven-days-a-week preaching mission whereby the pulpit and the pew put into practice the gospel enunciated each Sunday in the church. For after all is said and done, the impact of the church upon the life of our times will be made through the influence of a community of Christians preaching and living the Word of God faithfully in all of the significant areas of life. Baptists, perhaps more than most other Christian denominations, are in a favorable position to emphasize the total impact of the community of believers upon the world of sin and confusion. For the ministry of a Baptist church is not solely the responsibility of the man who has been ordained by a congregation; it is rather the extension of the mind and heart of Christ, the head of the church, through his body which is composed of pastor and people alike.

QUESTIONS FOR DISCUSSION

1. In what ways are standards for ordination a protection to the churches and to the ideal for the Christian ministry which it is the responsibility of the churches to safeguard?

2. In what ways can faulty placement procedures threaten the spiritual welfare of the churches? Would the development of an accepted procedure rob the churches of their right to govern themselves and to call their own ministers?

3. In what ways can ministers and laymen guide into the ministry young men and women who are superior in spirituality and in skills for leadership? Would this hinder the work of the Holy Spirit in calling a young man or woman into the ministry?

PROJECT SUGGESTIONS

1. List in your *Notebook of Facts* an analysis of your own local church, indicating what procedures are followed in recruitment of young people for Christian service, in ordination, in the calling of a pastor, in support of a college or seminary which is training ministers, and in lifting the salary scale of the minister.

2. Write an essay of one hundred words on "The Ministry I Should Like to See for Tomorrow."

SUPPLEMENTARY MATERIAL

1

Isaac Backus: Spokesman for Freedom

AGAINST THE BACKGROUND of the Great Awakening which swept like a prairie fire over New England in the 1730's and '40's, there emerged a tall young man of serious demeanor and modesty who was destined to be one of the great Baptist statesmen of all times. In his experience and faith he embodied all of the essentials of the Baptist witness. For that reason his legacy to us is significant, although all too few who benefit from it today know even his name, much less his accomplishments.

Isaac Backus was of venerable New England stock. His grandfather, Joseph Backus, was a justice of the peace in Norwich, Connecticut, and the town's representative in the legislative assembly of the colony. He was a man of deep convictions about his church life. As a Congregationalist, he remained true, all of his life, to the basic principles of his faith. For that reason, he opposed the Saybrook Platform which he regarded as a violation of Christian democracy because it placed authority for ecclesiastical matters in the hands of a synod of ministers and laymen.

Isaac's father, Samuel, was a prosperous farmer who had little to do with public affairs. He was a kindly husband and father. However, he did not make a profession of his Christian faith until four years prior to his death in 1740. Isaac's mother, Elizabeth, was a woman of deep piety, and she exercised the chief religious influence upon the lad. She dated her conversion from 1721, when she was twenty-three years of age. All through her life she matured in her Christian experience and talked freely with her neighbors about salvation.

Isaac was but sixteen years of age when George Whitefield in 1740 made his first tour of New England. Within a period of about two or three years, some thirty or forty thousand per-

81

sons were converted.[1] Strong emotionalism accompanied the
meetings, and many became so overcome by excitement that
they fell to the ground in a dead faint. Teen-aged Isaac Backus
attended the meetings and developed an anguish of soul, but it
brought no decision. Later he wrote concerning those trying
days—when he seemed to confuse emotional ecstasy with sound
conversion—these words: "But I had so much doctrinal knowledge, that I never was overcome in that manner. Neither could
I put off my concern, as I had done before, for a more con-
venient season."[2] There followed, during that summer, a
period of deep soul-concern. When, in August, James Daven-
port came to Norwich and people were being converted at his
meetings, Isaac became more tormented than ever, because he
"remained a hardened sinner."

Then one day, as he was mowing alone in the field, his entire
life seemed to open before him and he came under deep conviction. Seating himself in the shade of a tree, he saw more
clearly than ever his own sin and came to realize that if he did
not yield, God had a right to condemn him. His own words are
of interest, for they best describe the nature of that sacred
experience:

> My soul yielded all into His hands, fell at His feet, and was silent
> and calm before Him. . . . The Word of God and the promises of His
> Grace appeared firmer than a rock, and I was astonished at my pre-
> vious unbelief. My heavy burden was gone, tormenting fears were fled,
> and my joy was unspeakable.[3]

At first he was not sure that this moment of decision was
conversion, for he had conceived of that experience as one of
emotional ecstasy. But two days later he heard a sermon de-
scribing the inner witness. This sermon set his mind at ease.
For he realized that the evidence of a new life in Christ was
his experience of "a spirit of prayer, hatred of sin, overcoming
of the world, love to the brethren, and love to enemies."[4]

Now that he had yielded to Christ, the question of church
membership became uppermost in his thinking. At first, he was

[1] Trumbull, *History of Connecticut*, II, p. 263.
[2] Alvah Hovey, *A Memoir of the Life and Times of the Reverend Isaac Backus*
(Boston, 1859), p. 37.
[3] *Ibid.*, p. 39.
[4] *Ibid.*, p. 40.

loath to request admittance to the "regular" church of Norwich (the established Congregational church) because the pastor, Mr. Lord, was lax in maintaining church discipline and because the church admitted members without a written account of "a change of heart." However, after ten months, he so much desired to partake of the Lord's Supper that he set his scruples aside and, on July 11, 1742, united with that church, concluding, as he quaintly put it, "to bear those things as a burden and to hope for a reformation." [5] But the changes did not come; and so, early in 1745, he and a few others withdrew to hold separate services. When in August they were summoned before the church to explain their reasons, they stated them clearly: persons were allowed into membership without giving satisfactory evidence of conversion; there was a lax discipline of members; the pastor favored the Saybrook Platform, which had been renounced by the church before calling him; the preaching lacked emphasis upon conversion and experiential religion; and the pastor assailed many things of which they approved, including preaching by uneducated men. On October 17 they were suspended from membership, and on July 6, 1746, they organized their own church.

Actually, Backus and his little group were not peculiar in their stand. They were, indeed, a part of a movement of Separate or New Light churches that opposed the very things which Backus had objected to at Norwich. For our history the significant thing about his step is that he had moved in the direction of the Baptist view of the church as a company of regenerate believers. However, the final step of rejecting the covenant concept of the church held by Congregationalists was not taken immediately. In fact, it was as a New Light or Separate Congregationalist that Backus became a minister of the gospel.

Soon after the organization of the Separate Church in Norwich, he was attending a meeting in a home where the command was read, "Pray ye the Lord of the harvest that he will send forth laborers into his harvest." He reports: "A conviction seized my mind that God had given me abilities which his church had a right to the use of, and which I could not withhold

[5] *Ibid.*, p. 42.

with a clear conscience." [6] A few days later, his pastor, Mr. Hyde, invited him to go to Colchester and Lyme, where a revival was in process. On the journey, two persons were converted. He returned home rejoicing. The next day, September 27, 1746, at the age of twenty-two, alone in the woods, he realized that God had called him to preach, although it might mean, as he stated it, "reproaches, losses, imprisonment, and death." With the divine promise burning in his consciousness, "My grace is sufficient for thee," he preached the next day, which was Sunday, with ready approval of the church.

Isaac Backus' view of the ministry, even this early, was typical of that of the Baptists. At a time when the Congregational establishment made educational qualifications the primary requirement for ordination and standing in the ministry, he insisted that "all true ministers of the gospel are called into that work by the special influences of the Holy Spirit." [7] He denied, however, that his stress upon an inner call of God as the prime requisite invalidated the need for external ordination. He felt that one must have a visible standing in the visible church.

For the first fourteen months of his ministry, he itinerated in various towns of Connecticut, Rhode Island, and Massachusetts, managing to escape prosecution, although the law of 1742 prohibited preaching in Connecticut by one not settled or an ordained minister. In December, 1747, he was introduced to Titicut parish in Massachusetts, where he was to labor for more than half a century. It was comprised of Bridgewater on the north, and a part of Middleborough on the south of the Taunton River, which separated the towns. On February 16, 1748, a Separate Church (Congregational) was organized, and on March 31 its members, thirty-four in number, gave Backus a unanimous call. He accordingly was ordained on April 13, at the age of twenty-six. His diffidence and lack of more than elementary education bothered him. But very soon he gained a certain freedom in preaching, which he called a "freedom of the Spirit." Although he never acquired any great facility in sermonizing, not having developed early in life a disciplined and

---

[6] *Ibid.,* p. 60.

[7] Isaac Backus, "Discourse on the Nature and Necessity of an Internal Call to Preach the Everlasting Gospel," cited in Hovey, *op. cit.,* p. 62.

logical mind, he read deeply and widely in theology, church history, and polity. By his characteristic diligence and careful economizing of time, he combined the work of a traveling evangelist with that of a pastoral ministry and with ever-accumulating public responsibilities.

The year 1749 is significant for two reasons. First, he married a charming and helpful lady by the name of Susanna Mason of Rehoboth, with whom he shared his life and ministry for fifty-one years. Second, he undertook a study of the doctrine of baptism. This became necessary when contention arose in his church over two members who embraced the principle of believer's baptism. At first, Backus sought to remain neutral, but on August 20 he determined to prepare a sermon on the issue for the following Sunday. His study of the Bible during the week led him to interpret Romans 6:4, which was to be his text, according to the Baptist principle that none but believers have a right to baptism and that immersion is the only correct mode.

Although he preached his sermon, he was greatly disturbed in mind during the following days. On September 26 he retracted the sermon at the Tuesday meeting of the church. For two years thereafter he grappled with the question: "Where, and in what relation to the church of God, do those stand who have been baptized and yet are not believers?" Finally, he set Saturday, July 20, 1751, as a day of secret fasting and prayer to find God's will in the matter. On July 25 he announced to his church that he had become convinced that there is no Scriptural warrant for infant baptism, that the church is not a body of those received from birth into the covenant, but a fellowship of those who have voluntarily sought entrance into it upon a profession of their personal faith in Jesus Christ as Lord and Savior. On August 22, 1751, he was baptized with six members of his church by Elder Benjamin Pierce of Warwick, Rhode Island.

Although he had no intention of leaving his church, his act caused offense. As a result, conferences were held between Separate Congregational churches and Baptists concerning the practice of intercommunion. Because they had much in common and shared the evangelistic zeal of the Awakening, both desired union. However, a tenseness of relationships developed within the church, as both groups sought to avoid reference to the subject of baptism and refrained from partaking of the Lord's Supper together. Others left the church. Backus sought to practice open membership and invited a Congregationalist minister from outside to baptize infants. Finally, it became clear that separation was the only solution, so on January 16, 1756, Backus and the six who had been baptized with him met at his home to organize a Baptist church. He was installed as its pastor on June 23. The final step had been taken in his spiritual pilgrimage to discover the will of God for his life, as he sought to be true to the New Testament.

The price he had paid in soul-searching and in abuse from those who did not agree with him undoubtedly contributed to making Isaac Backus the foremost Baptist statesman in behalf of religious liberty. With him this principle was a deep conviction. From his youth he had witnessed the injustice of the established church in imposing itself upon those of another persuasion. He had seen Baptists forced to pay a tax to support the established minister in the community, when they had barely enough money to provide their own ministry. He had seen courageous farmers refuse to pay their tax for conscience' sake, only to forfeit their plow, their livestock, or their crop. He was familiar also with the humiliating experience to which these people were subjected, after 1757, by the certificate laws which forced a Baptist, if he would be exempted from paying the hateful tax, to prove his good standing in his church by securing three signatures of members of the church to which he belonged.

In March, 1771, Backus wrote a letter to the General Assembly of Massachusetts Bay Colony "concerning taxes to support religious worship." In September, 1772, the Warren Association of Baptist churches chose him to be their agent in behalf of their liberties in place of John Davis, who had died. For more than ten years he served with a committee of eight in this capacity, writing appeals, sending petitions to the General Court of Massachusetts, and keeping the Baptists of the other colonies and those in England informed. In fact, his work was not unlike that of the present executive director of the Baptist Joint Committee on Public Affairs in Washington, D. C.

His efforts were often maligned by his enemies. Soon after his trip to Philadelphia to appear with other Baptists before a committee of the First Continental Congress in September, 1774, to plead for religious freedom, Robert Treat Paine of the Massachusetts delegation spread the rumor that Backus had gone to Philadelphia to prevent the colonies from uniting in defense of their liberties.

When the Episcopalians were agitating for a resident bishop in America, who would, of course, have been supported by the state, Backus underscored his protest with a statement which summarizes his principle:

The plain truth is, by the Gospel-charter, all professed Christians are vested with precisely the same rights; nor has one denomination any more right to the interposition of the civil magistrate in their favor than another; and whenever this difference takes place, it is beside the rule of *Scripture,* and I may say also, the genuine dictates of *uncorrupted reason.*[8]

With equal vigor he defended the American Revolution and outlined in his history of the Baptists in New England five reasons for their support of the war, among which he emphasized the fact that the worst treatment that had been accorded the Baptists in America had come from the practice of the same principles that had caused the Revolution.[9]

Largely through the efforts of Backus and his committee, the cause of religious liberty, unpalatable as it was to the establishment, was kept before the people of New England and the country at large. When the Revolution finally came to its close, the Baptists, who had participated almost to a man, had gained much favor in the public mind. The prestige of their ministers and churches had risen in New England to such an extent that by 1795 few dared to prosecute any Baptist who refused to pay the tax for the support of the state church. It was not until 1833, however, that church and state were separated in Massachusetts, the last of the states to yield to the principle which was to safeguard religious liberty.

With the same zeal and vigor that had characterized his early

[8] Hovey, *op. cit.,* p. 235.

[9] Isaac Backus, *A History of New England with Particular Reference to the Denomination of Christians called Baptists.* Second ed., 2 vols. (Newton, Mass., 1871), II, pp. 197-98.

years, Backus rounded out a long ministry. Year after year he preached an average of two hundred sermons, one-half of them in private homes. In 1788, when he was sixty-four years of age, he was selected by the Warren Association to go to Virginia in response to a call for "ministerial aid from the north." He sailed from Newport on January 2, 1789, and after a very rough voyage, landed at Washington in Beaufort County, North Carolina, about noon on January 10. There he found a few brethren, preached, and moved on, holding meetings as he went. He spoke almost every day in meetinghouses, courthouses, or dwelling houses. "Between January 10 and May 27 he traveled on horseback twelve hundred and fifty-one miles in North Carolina and Virginia, and preached one hundred and seventeen sermons." [10] In addition to his preaching, he gave counsel in the settlement of ecclesiastical difficulties, and he found time as he traveled to gather material for the second volume of his history.

After fifty-eight years as pastor at Titicut, he suffered a stroke in March, 1806, and died on November 20, at the age of eighty-two years and ten months. His intimate friend, Dr. Thomas Baldwin, said of him, "He was a burning and shining light."

For a lifetime he had combined the work of evangelist, pastor, and defender of religious freedom, because he believed with all his being in the New Testament concept of vital personal faith in a democratic church life. It was truly said of him that "he was a great Christian statesman and a courageous spokesman for freedom."

[10] Hovey, *op. cit.*, p. 272.

2

John Mason Peck: Builder of Men and Institutions

JOHN MASON PECK passed away quietly at a quarter before nine on Sunday evening, March 14, 1858. During the day he had said to an old friend, "Only Christ is my Savior, my whole dependence." Many remarked later that these last words expressed better than anything else the secret of his life. Two days afterward, he was buried in Rock Spring Cemetery near the scenes of his earliest labors in the West—in the West that knew and loved him as "the Old Pioneer." An old associate in the work, the Rev. James Lemen, preached on the text: "I have fought a good fight, I have finished the course, I have kept the faith." Twenty-nine days later they removed his body to the Bellefontaine Cemetery in St. Louis and erected a shaft of white marble as a memorial of the man who had spent his life pointing men to God.

He had had little advantage of formal training, yet to him Harvard University awarded in 1852 the honorary degree of Doctor of Systematic Theology in recognition of a life devoted to Christian education. He had never held a public office, yet the historian, Evarts Boutell Greene, could say of him: "He was beyond question one of the strongest forces for intelligence and righteousness in the whole Mississippi Valley." [1] He never claimed to be other than a humble missionary of Jesus Christ, yet more than a century after his death, his biographer, in commenting on his death, could write without exaggeration the following tribute:

So went out the light of one of the most useful lives that the Mississippi Valley has ever known. For forty years John Mason Peck lived in the valley, seeing and helping largely to direct the onward progress of western civilization. In missions, in Sunday schools, in temperance and educational work he was a pioneer; in newspaper work and authorship he achieved nation-wide fame; in every line tending to social achievement he was a leader. [2]

[1] Greene, *Pioneers of Civilization in Illinois* (1907), cited in Matthew Lawrence, *John Mason Peck: The Pioneer Missionary* (New York, 1940), p. 12.

[2] Lawrence, *op. cit.*, p. 107.

We may well ask the question: What is the key to the greatness of such a man? To provide an answer, in part at least, is
the purpose of this presentation.

It is to be found, first of all, in the fact that he had sur-
rendered all to Jesus Christ. The consuming passion of his life
from the moment of his conversion was to do the will of his
Savior, which for him was to establish the kingdom of God on
the frontiers of the expanding West.

He was the product of six generations of sturdy New England stock. His father, Asa Peck, was a farmer who wrested
from the rocky soil of Litchfield, Connecticut, a living too scant
to provide his only son with more than a few winters of the
most elementary education. Yet at eighteen years of age, in
order to supplement the family income, John began to teach the
children of the community. Even that early, he manifested the
positive personality, the clear mind, the excellent common
sense, and the high purpose that was to characterize his entire
life.

His spiritual awakening came in December of that same year
(1807), when, out of curiosity, he attended revival services in
the town. He later described his experience in his diary: "My
burden became heavier, until the end of the week, when I was
delivered, and found a peace of mind and a joy in God which
I had never felt before." [3] Although he felt, at the time, some
inclination to enter Christian service, his high concept of the
ministry and its requirement of training held him back from
answering the call until four years later.

In the meantime, he was married on May 8, 1809, to Miss
Sally Paine of Greene County, New York, who was living with
her grandparents in Litchfield. She, too, had been converted in
the revival services held in December, 1807. So, together, they
united with the Congregational Church in Litchfield. When their
first child was born, they sought counsel about his baptism. Not
being convinced of the scriptural character of infant baptism,
they refrained from presenting him for the sacrament. Then,
in the spring of 1811 they moved to Windham, in Greene
County, New York. By this time, they were thinking seriously

---

[3] Austen K. deBlois and Lemuel Call Barnes, *John Mason Peck and One Hundred
Years of Home Missions, 1817-1917* (New York, 1917), p. 10.

of becoming Baptists. The nearest church of that denomination was at New Durham, five miles by path over the mountain. One Sunday in August they made the trip, and soon they were baptized and received into its membership.

By October, Peck was ready to present himself for the ministry. After the manner of the times, the church voted that he should "improve his gift," and arranged for him to preach to the congregation on Sunday, the thirteenth. His text was prophetic of the ministry that lay before him: "And he said unto them, Go ye into all the world, and preach the gospel to every creature" (Mark 16:15). Thus, at twenty-two years of age, he began a ministry which was to last for forty-six years.

After being licensed to preach, he accepted in 1812 a call to the pastorate of the Baptist church at Catskill, New York. To earn his living he taught school, for the offerings from the three services which he conducted each week averaged only about one dollar. On June 9, 1813, the church ordained him. Six months later, he accepted a call to the church in Amenia. There also he sought to supplement his income by teaching school. Meanwhile, he sought to improve himself by study under the direction of Principal Barnes of the Dutchess Academy in Poughkeepsie.

It was at Amenia that he first heard Luther Rice speak; this was at the Warwick Association in June, 1815. Peck, thoroughly inspired, invited him to his home, where the two young men talked far into the night about missions. The result was that Rice offered Peck the responsibility of visiting certain associations in central New York in behalf of foreign missions.

During that first year of promotional work, Peck organized auxiliary missionary societies and traveled hundreds of miles on horseback. Impressed by the importance of this wider ministry, he resigned his church at the end of the year, and three months later he closed his school.

At the time of his resignation he wrote to Rice, asking five specific questions: (1) Is it contemplated to form a permanent mission station in the West? (2) Would it be best to have schools connected with the mission? (3) Is there any place in view for the seat of the mission? (4) What literary attainments would be indispensable? (5) Would it be thought necessary for some person to accompany you on your prospective western tour? Rice's replies were right to the point: To questions 1 and 2, the answer was "Yes." To number 3, it was "St. Louis, probably." To number 4, the answer was "A good English education and as much more as possible." And to number 5, "Yes, if the person in question is ready to offer himself as a missionary, and go West *for life.*" [4]

The die was cast. Peck accepted the challenge. In April, leaving his wife and children for a time in Litchfield, he went to Philadelphia to study for a year with Dr. Staughton, pastor of the Sansom Street Baptist Church, who had five pupils in his home preparing for the ministry. One of them was James E. Welch, who was later to become Peck's associate as a missionary to the West. This was a busy and a valuable year. Peck preached almost every Sunday. During his summer vacation, he made an evangelistic tour of parts of New Jersey. He studied the Sunday school methods which were then being introduced in Philadelphia. He talked with prisoners and with poor people in the slums.

His day began at 6 A.M. with private prayer, an hour of Bible study, and then regular study of assigned work until breakfast. After breakfast, he received instruction in Latin, Greek, natural philosophy, and the use of globes and astronomy, composition of sermons, theology, and medicine. Evenings were spent in study of the classics, writing, and copying. He closed the day with another hour of Bible reading. It was, indeed, an intensive course into which Peck entered as a mature man who was consumed with a profound sense of mission.

When, in May, 1817, the Triennial Convention met in Philadelphia to undertake home missions and a school, in addition to the responsibility it already had for foreign missions, Peck and Welsh were appointed as missionaries to the West. The instructions given them were very specific: (1) Begin at St. Louis or in its vicinity. (2) Establish a school or schools there. (3) Collect scattered brethren into churches. (4) And in particular, work with the Fox, Osage, Kansas, and other tribes of Indians. A thousand dollars was appropriated for their journey to St. Louis, but no guarantee was made for their continuing support.

---

[4] Rufus Babcock, *Memoir of John Mason Peck, D.D.* (Philadelphia, 1864), pp. 49-50.

It was, therefore, completely by an act of faith that Peck and his family left Litchfield on July 28, 1817, in a one-horse wagon.

The trip from Connecticut to St. Louis, now traversed in little more than twenty-four hours by train, took Peck and his family 129 days. From Litchfield to Philadelphia required ten days. After a week or so in the city, they set out across Pennsylvania, a journey which required a month. After three weeks in Ohio, they recrossed the Ohio River into Kentucky on October 23. On November 6, they crossed the Ohio River a third time and landed in Illinois Territory at Shawneetown. There Peck preached his first sermon, selecting as his text Acts 13:26: "Men and brethren, children of the stock of Abraham, and whosoever among you feareth God, to you is the word of this salvation sent." After twenty-two days journey up the Mississippi River, they arrived in St. Louis, Peck being at the time ill with pneumonia, from which he did not recover for two months.

The problems confronting him would have defeated a man of less courage. In St. Louis, prices were so greatly inflated that he and his wife and three children were obliged to live in a single room which once had been an accountant's office. The population of the frontier town was Anglo-American, French, and African. Some were floaters, people of the worst sort who spent their time in violence and vice. Many of them were blasphemous infidels who mocked the Lord's Supper, burned Bibles, shouted prayers and hymns irreverently, and insisted that "the Sabbath shall never cross the Mississippi." Others were settlers who were professional men, government officials, storekeepers, Indian traders—mostly honest and respectable people, although prone to use their spare time for drinking and gambling. There were a few earnest Christians. Less than a month before Peck's arrival, the first Presbyterian church established in the West beyond the Mississippi had been organized.

Peck and Welch could never have succeeded in the face of such obstacles without a complete surrender to Christ and an all-consuming missionary passion. Illustrative of the fortitude and cheerfulness with which Peck faced the hardships involved are two paragraphs taken from his journal:

Eating was not so very important; for any man in the vigor of life in those days in this frontier country, who could not go without food for twenty-four hours, and more especially a preacher of the gospel, ought to be sent back where he came from, to the kind care of his friends.

This is followed by directions for spending a comfortable night in the open.

The first thing is to select the right place in some hollow or ravine protected from the wind, and if possible behind some old forest giant which the storms of winter have prostrated. And then, reader, don't build your fire against the tree, for this is the place for your head and shoulders to lie, and around which the smoke and heated air may curl. Then don't be so childish as to lie on the wet or cold frozen earth, without a bed. Gather a quantity of grass, leaves, and small brush, and after you have cleared away the snow, and provided for protection from the wet or cold earth, you may sleep comfortably. If you have a piece of jerked venison, and a bit of pone with a cup of water, you may make out a splendid supper, provided you think so, "for as a man thinketh, so is he."[5]

The key to an understanding of the greatness of John Mason Peck lies not only in his complete surrender to his Savior, but also in the fact that he was consciously planning and building for the ages. In 1824 he wrote to the Massachusetts Baptist Missionary Society:

My mind is often deeply impressed with the thought that I am laboring for future generations, and that the principles inculcated and the habits introduced in the Baptist Society in this country will last for ages. Under what high and weighty responsibility should every professor, and particularly every preacher, act who lays the foundation in a new country.[6]

It was always the challenge of the larger issues which attracted Peck's interest and concern. While he spent a lifetime working with people and local congregations, he never allowed his mind and heart to be limited to the purely local.

His great wisdom in this respect is seen in the manner in which he endeavored to meet the problems which faced him during that first year in St. Louis. The Foreign Mission Board, it will be recalled, had been particularly desirous that he and Welch should give their energies to work among the Indians.

[5] *Ibid.*, p. 104.
[6] Lawrence, *op. cit.*, p. 37.

But Peck saw that such work would avail but little, if the white settlers were not converted, organized into strong churches, and led to support a leadership adequate to include the wider ministry in their responsibilities.

Therefore, from the first, he began a program which included itinerant preaching, personal soul-winning, and the establishing of schools. In a room in the rear of a store (14 x 16 feet) which he and Welch rented for fourteen dollars a month, a preaching station and a school were soon developed. The school had, within a year, forty paying pupils, ten free of charge who were chiefly French Catholics, and one hundred Negro children.

Peck was a strong advocate of education. Wherever he went, he inquired how the needs of the people were being met. He strongly opposed the ignorant and "whiskey drinking Irishmen" who had control of three-fourths of the frontier schools. In their place, he recommended the well-trained young men from New England.

One of the marks of Peck's genius on the frontier was his understanding of the principle that if you want to have permanent results, you must follow your preaching by giving the people something to do. He saw the importance of leaving in each community a continuing organization and program. This was always his practice. When, in October, 1818, he visited the Bethel Association, which was composed of a handful of struggling Baptist churches of Missouri and Arkansas Territory in the vicinity of Cape Girardeau, Missouri, he brought forth a plan whereby: (1) the association might enter into correspondence with the Board of Missions through its corresponding secretary; (2) the churches which desired might affiliate with a new society to be organized in the vicinity; (3) a new constitution could be adopted that would set up an organization or society to aid the Western Mission in spreading the gospel and providing elementary schools for whites and Indians; (4) anyone of good moral character could become a member by paying five dollars a year, while each Baptist association which contributed to the work could send two missionaries to the annual meetings; (5) teachers were to be paid by the communities, but worthy students for the ministry or a profession were to be given assistance by the new society; and (6) teachers were to be secured from the East. The plan was adopted by the Illinois Association on October 10, and by the Missouri Association on October 24. It thus established the first society of any denomination to be organized west of the Mississippi for philanthropic or missionary purposes. So effective was it that within three years after its formation, more than fifty good schools were established in Missouri and Illinois.[7]

Most of the people amongst whom Peck worked, according to his own description, were "ignorant; few could read, and fewer families had Bibles." They knew no missionaries; they had no idea why the church should minister to those beyond its own circle. They had little ambition, even in their farming. Their venison, bear meat, and pork were dressed and cooked in a slovenly and filthy manner. Not one woman in ten knew how to cook tea and coffee, even if these commodities had been available. Cornbread was the staple food. They were living, Peck says, " a kind of half-savage life."

His efforts to remedy this situation were specific: (1) He organized on December 9, 1818, a Missouri Bible Society affiliated with the American Bible Society. (2) He formed branch Bible societies in local communities. (3) He established schools, as we have seen. (4) He introduced the Bible into public schools as a text for regular reading. (5) He organized Sunday schools which were linked up with the "Philadelphia Sunday and Adult School Union," the progenitor of the American Sunday School Union, which was not organized until 1824. By September, 1825, he had one hundred Sunday schools in operation with 3,000 scholars. (6) He organized women's support of his program by establishing "Female Mite Societies" to pay the missionaries who traveled and preached in the more destitute regions. (7) He saw the need for a trained ministry, and established a school of high grade at St. Charles (twenty miles northeast of St. Louis), called St. Charles Academy; it was conducted by himself and Rev. James Craig of Ohio.

In 1820, the Triennial Convention abruptly stopped its support of the Western Mission. This was largely because their interest was absorbed in foreign missions, funds were lacking,

---

[7] deBlois, *op. cit.*, pp. 34-35.

[8] *Ibid.*, p. 37.

and there was criticism that the home mission project did not devote itself sufficiently to the Indians. Peck, undaunted, carried on alone until 1822, when he was appointed by the Massachusetts Baptist Missionary Society. His income was to be only five dollars a week while actually in the field. He was obliged to earn his own salary.

In April, therefore, he moved to Rock Spring, Illinois, where he settled on a half-section of land, part of which he farmed for a living. In the vicinity he found some Georgia Baptists who had sat under the ministry of Dr. Jesse Mercer. These he organized into a church. Illinois became the center of his labors. To its communities he came to be known as "the Pioneer." He utilized four agencies to accomplish his work: (1) sermons; (2) Bibles, Testaments, tracts, and pamphlets—as many as his horse could carry; the Bibles he sold, the tracts he distributed free of charge; (3) Sunday schools; and (4) personal conversations. When he evangelized, he established Sunday schools, always with great dignity, planning, and advance promotion.

Peck discounted an evangelism that was bereft of Christian education. He was skeptical of the emotional excitement of camp meetings, which he felt "might have been produced without the agency of God, and might be and seemed to be only the effect of human causes." [9] Although a staunch Baptist, he manifested no narrowness or bigotry toward other denominations. Frequently he visited Methodist Camp Meetings and Presbyterian Conferences. Indeed, his Bible societies were all organized on an interdenominational basis.

The breadth of Peck's conception of a Christian leader's work is indicated also by the numerous causes to which he gave his attention. He was agent of the Colonization Society for Negroes; he was a stalwart advocate of temperance. He studied the problems of immigrants carefully and published, in 1831, a *Guide to Emigrants*. He strongly opposed slavery and led in the organizing of the antislavery forces of Illinois in the 1820's, when the slavery men were endeavoring to change the constitution to admit slavery in that state. And always he was the proponent of education.

In fact, it was to arouse the zeal of Baptists in the East for

[9] *Ibid.*, p. 55.

the evangelization of the West and to explain the necessity of a trained ministry and an educated citizenship that Peck, in 1826, traveled East. He reached Boston in time for the annual meeting of the Massachusetts Baptist Missionary Society. To them he presented a Master Plan which called for three things: (1) the support of circuit preachers in the western states, who were to be paid one hundred dollars a year by the Board, the rest of their salary to be raised by the churches on the field; (2) the appointment of a strong minister at St. Louis, who would be a pastor and develop a school; and (3) the founding of a theological school in Illinois. In pleading for this third point, Peck said to the Board:

> I cannot bear that our preachers in Illinois and Missouri should continue as ignorant as some of them are. In the three states are not less than 250 Baptist preachers. A majority of them have been raised on the frontiers, with scarcely the advantages of a common school education, and not even habituated to read the word of God in early life. Every year is adding to the number of this class of preachers. . . . What should be done? Is not the path of duty plain as the noonday sun? Furnish these men with the means of school education as circumstances admit. Establish a theological school.[10]

The Board adopted his plans, and he set out to raise the funds.

Returning to Rock Spring with nearly one thousand dollars, he undertook the building of the new school. To save money, he worked with his own hands at laying the foundation and cutting poles for the frame of the building. One day while he was so engaged, a young Presbyterian minister, John M. Ellis, rode by. He had but lately come to Illinois, and was a graduate of Andover Theological Seminary. Inquiring of Peck what he was doing, he obtained the reply, "I am building a theological seminary." Ellis exclaimed, "What, in these barrens?" "Yes," said Peck, "I am planting the seed." During the conversation that followed, Peck suggested that the Presbyterians ought to be doing something toward college and theological education. The suggestion developed in Ellis' mind; and in time he was instrumental in the founding of Illinois College at Jacksonville." [11]

[10] deBlois, op. cit., p. 61.
[11] Lawrence, John Mason Peck, p. 52.

By November 1, 1827, the Rock Spring Theological and High School opened. During the four years that it was continued, the enrollment reached 130 students. But the strain of administering the school without secure financial backing was too much for Peck. So, in 1831, the trustees closed it until a better location (one nearer a small city) could be found, and until proper support could be obtained. In June of that year, Dr. Jonathan Going of Worcester, Massachusetts, a faithful supporter of the Western Mission in the East, arrived at Rock Spring. For three months, he and Peck explored a large part of Indiana, Illinois, Missouri, and Kentucky, planning for the future.

When the two men parted at Shelbyville, Kentucky, in September, two important decisions had been made. The site of the seminary was to be Upper Alton and a plan had been devised for the organization of the American Baptist Home Mission Society. In 1832, both plans came to fruition. The new school, known as Alton College, was opened in September. It was later renamed Shurtleff College to honor one of its chief benefactors, a Boston physician who contributed, in 1835, the sum of ten thousand dollars. Peck became in the same year the first appointee of the new Home Mission Society.

The man who had founded churches, established Sunday schools and Bible societies, and had organized a theological school and college also saw the importance of a religious newspaper. Although Peck was opposed vigorously in this project, even by his firmest supporters, he began, in April, 1829, the publication of *The Pioneer of the Valley of the Mississippi.* Frequently, he found it necessary to pay the debts incurred out of his own meager earnings from the farm or the sale of his books. In 1839, the paper, then known as the *Western Pioneer,* was removed to Kentucky, where it was united with the *Baptist Banner* and given the name, *Banner and Pioneer.*

In that year Peck was fifty years of age and exhausted from the strain of vigorous activities, strenuous travel, and the weight of great responsibilities of leadership. For a time he felt that he must retire, but with the coming year he took fresh courage.

In 1841 his keenness of judgment was tested to the full, for the convention of Western Baptists, meeting at Louisville in June, made a great effort to separate from the eastern societies.

In order to avoid the rupture, which had grown out of a feeling of remoteness from the eastern agencies, Peck supported a compromise measure, the organization of the Western Baptist Publication and Sunday School Society as an affiliate of the American Baptist Publication Society. Having staved off the break, Peck went East to talk plainly to the Publication Board in Philadelphia about their inefficiency, petty jealousies, and inability to exert their powers for bigger things. They applauded his speech, but went about their narrow tasks.

It had been Peck's purpose to make them see the missionary opportunity which they had in the South and the West. In line with this purpose, he sought to bring Philadelphia, New York, and Boston, together with the newer cities of Louisville, New Orleans, St. Louis, and Chicago, in a national society that would spread the knowledge of the Bible and of religious literature and thus develop denominational solidarity in matters of faith and practice. For six months he struggled in the East with this problem. For his pains, he was accused by the western Baptists of favoring the Philadelphia Society, while the eastern Baptists withheld full co-operation because they were more concerned with the foreign and home mission societies. To be sure, they had no objection to the existence of two publication societies, which they regarded as self-sufficient agencies. What they failed to see was that a single, strong publication society was necessary to undergird the entire denominational program.

In February, 1843, while the problems were still mounting, Peck was elected secretary of the American Baptist Publication Society. He accepted when assured that he might undertake a program designed to effect economies and to make more efficient the operations of the society. In that manner he hoped that the Society would inspire the confidence of the denomination. He arrived in Philadelphia on April 17, and went to work at once. With the churches, he used two methods: he described the great need, and he appealed to Baptist loyalty to meet the situation in a noble and effective way. At the very outset, he met with two difficulties: the foreign mission society's debt of $40,000 and the current antislavery contention. Nevertheless, he accomplished much. He visited repeatedly nearly all of the eastern, middle, and southern states. He planned a system of branch depositories. He enlarged the staff of agents and colporteurs. He increased each year the contributions from the churches. By his Christian spirit, he kept the northern and southern churches together for a while longer in their support of the Society. In May, 1846, he felt that he must resign and return to his beloved prairies and home.[12]

During the next several years, until his death in 1858, his influence continued to be felt through his heavy correspondence, his literary work, his lectures and addresses. In April, 1852, he visited Philadelphia once again, and submitted a plan to the American Baptist Publication Society for the organizing of a Baptist Historical Society, which was adopted. Once again, he had laid the foundation for an agency which is still in existence.

In the same year, Harvard awarded him the honorary degree of Doctor of Systematic Theology. He was rich, indeed, in the acclaim of men, but terribly poor in financial reserves. Then, on November 18, came the heartbreaking fire which destroyed the Rock Spring Seminary building in which were housed some eight to ten thousand volumes of his libraries. Fortunately, however, his diaries, journals, correspondence, association minutes, and the books he used most were safe in his home.

In 1856 his wife died, without whose help, he says, he "could not have made half the sacrifices and performed half the services kind friends have attributed to me." [13] On Sunday, March 14, 1858, after long days of suffering, he himself was called to his eternal reward.

Few men have left so rich a legacy to posterity as John Mason Peck. Almost singlehanded, he shaped the life of the great Baptist work that stands as a memorial to his labors in the Middle West. He was the moulder of two of the major societies of American Baptists: the American Baptist Home Mission Society and the American Baptist Publication Society. Through his labors, he left the imprint of his vigorous Christian leadership upon the social and cultural life of a great section of the United States. Truly he was "a builder of men and of institutions." [14]

[12] See deBlois, *op. cit.*, pp. 91-98 and Lawrence, *op. cit.*, pp. 77-81.
[13] deBlois, *John Mason Peck*, pp. 106-07.
[14] *Ibid.*, p. 110.

3

Augustus Hopkins Strong: God's Interpreter

S TRONG, I wish you were a Christian." A young under-
graduate at Yale by the name of Wilder gathered enough
courage to speak these words to Augustus Strong, a classmate,
about his soul's salvation. Strong was a brilliant student with
a dignity and sureness of demeanor that caused his fellow students to stand in awe of him. But this friendly word from young
Wilder penetrated beneath his reserve and made him uncomfortable. It started a train of thought which prompted him, upon
his return to Rochester in his junior year, to attend the meetings
being conducted by Charles G. Finney. Although he did not
accept the evangelist's theology, he was stirred by his irresistible
logic and burning appeal to become a Christian.

At once, Strong knew that God wanted him in the ministry.
So, upon his graduation from Yale in 1857, he went to
Rochester Theological Seminary, from which he graduated two
years later. This was followed by two years abroad in study
at the University of Berlin and in travel in Germany. Upon
his return to America, he was called to the pastorate of the
First Baptist Church in Haverhill, Massachusetts, where he was
ordained on August 3, 1861. In 1865 he accepted a call to the
First Baptist Church in Cleveland, Ohio. It was during this
pastorate of six years that his daughter became acquainted with
John D. Rockefeller's eldest son, whom she later married. In
1872 Dr. Strong was elected to the presidency of Rochester
Theological Seminary, a post which he filled with outstanding
success for forty years.

In view of his background and start in the ministry, it is not
surprising that his career was significant for the denomination
which he served so faithfully. He was the descendant of John
Strong who came to Massachusetts in 1630 and distinguished
himself as a founder of Northampton. His father, Alvah Strong,
was for many years publisher of an influential up-State daily,

102

the *Rochester Democrat.* At the age of sixteen, Augustus was taken into his father's business office. Since his father was the first treasurer of Rochester Theological Seminary, Augustus became acquainted with the first generation of students in the institution to which he was to devote the major portion of his life. Not only were his home life and early contacts auspicious for his ministry, but his pastorates were such as to encourage his development as a scholarly preacher with keen theological discernment. From these facts it becomes evident that God was providentially preparing him for a most significant role in the development of American Baptists for more than half a century.

During that time he saw the Baptists increase in number from less than a million and a half to more than ten millions. He witnessed a broadening of their outlook and sense of mission in relation to other denominations. When he began his ministry, the Baptist fellowship was torn by dissension between North and South. Later he saw three great societies dominate Baptist affairs in the North for a generation (the American Baptist Foreign Mission Society, the American Baptist Home Mission Society, and the American Baptist Publication Society). He lived to see the Anniversaries, those annual gatherings of the various societies, give way to a concentration of separate interests in the Northern Baptist Convention which was organized in 1907. By Baptists generally, he came to be regarded as the interpreter of the old and the new in denominational thought and enterprise. Often his advice was accepted as the last word on important issues.

In a very true sense, therefore, he was for more than fifty years God's interpreter for Baptists. His books were read widely in both the North and the South. His theological thinking shaped the pattern of preaching during his long service as seminary president, and it has continued in influence to the present time in spite of the intrusion of a more liberal point of view after the First World War.

As an interpreter of God, Augustus Strong never lost sight of the importance of the church. All through his ministry, he maintained a fervent belief in the mystical union of Jesus Christ with the believer in an intimate and redemptive fellowship. His own personal relation to the church began on his twentieth

birthday, August 3, 1856, when he was baptized into the fellowship of the First Baptist Church of Rochester, New York. For
sixty-five years (with the exception of eleven years of absence
during pastorates in Haverhill and Cleveland) he maintained
his relationship with that church. He was always present Sunday mornings and evenings, and at midweek prayer meetings.
In the Sunday school he taught an adult class which came to
be known by his name. He was much in earnest about the
purity and spirituality of the church. He believed strongly in
evangelism, missions, and democracy in church life.

At a dinner of the Rochester Baptist Social Union, during
the seminary anniversaries of 1912 which marked the close of
his presidency, Dr. Strong spoke reminiscently and somewhat
autobiographically concerning his conversion and uniting with
the church. In the course of his remarks he said:

I made a compact with the Lord at the time, that I would serve him
in the way marked out in his Word. That Word seemed to indicate
that the church is founded by the Lord Jesus, redeemed by his blood
and regenerated by his Spirit. It is his appointed instrument for saving
men, and for that end is enlightened by his truth, united by his love,
and empowered by his Spirit. The church is Christ's representative in
the world, and therefore its life, its policy, its ordinances, are sacred.
Best of all, the church is the body, of which Christ is the head, the
soul, the life, so that each Christian can say: "Not I live, but Christ
liveth in me." His mystical and transcendent element in the church
makes it, next to Christ himself, the object of our love and service,
and in the final judgment our Lord recognizes service to his brethren
as service to himself. So I gave myself to Christ and his church.[1]

From the time that he became president of the Seminary in
1872, he emphasized the local church as the focal point of all
Christian work. All during his administration he maintained
a close relationship to the churches. In the address referred to
above, he expressed his view of the sacred responsibility of
maintaining this relationship:

I have tried to keep in touch with the churches, and to make the
Seminary useful to them. In an age of doubt and unrest I have endeavored to hold the Seminary true to the faith once for all delivered
to the saints, and to commit the truth to faithful men who should be
able to teach others also.[2]

[1] Augustus H. Strong *Memorial Number, The Rochester Theological Seminary
Bulletin: The Record* (May, 1922), pp. 58-59).
[2] *Ibid.*, p. 59.

Strong recognized in the churches the very nerve center of the progress of the kingdom of God.[3] It was through the local church, he believed, that the denomination would be magnified. He earnestly contended that if *the churches* were made "the custodians and interpreters of Christ," one need have no fear for *the Church of Christ*.[4]

As an interpreter of God, Strong never lost sight of the significance of the church; neither did he lose sight of the redemptive character of the gospel. A sampling of his sermon themes will illustrate this fact: "The Living God," "The Holiness of God," "The Two Natures of Christ," "The Necessity of the Atonement," "The Kingdom and Its Coming," and "The Greatness and Claims of Christ." Although his preaching was always strongly doctrinal in nature, he was sought after by churches, universities, conventions, and religious congresses. When the Baptist World Alliance met at its organization meeting in London in 1905, Augustus Strong was selected to preach the Congress Sermon.

He regarded his explanation of the method of the atonement as his specific contribution to theological science. And although he was criticized for his point of view that Christ could only become our Savior by actually taking our sinful nature as well as our guilt upon him, he defended his position to the last. He felt that there could be no deep imparting of the righteousness of Christ to believers through that mystical union with the Savior unless Christ had first of all identified himself with the sinful race of men.[5]

Even his acceptance of the hypothesis of evolution—and he was the first of American theologians to accept it—was fitted into his redemptive concept of the gospel. He interpreted evolution as the method of God. To him, it spelled divine purpose, the goal of which, for man, was Christ.[6]

Although he represented firmly the orthodox tradition in theology, he encouraged his students and faculty members to pursue their own researches in the entire realm of truth. In his

[3] *Ibid.,* p. 8.
[4] *Ibid.,* p. 30.
[5] *Augustus H. Strong Memorial Number,* pp. 56-57.
[6] *Ibid.,* p. 56.

own study, he made room for historical theology, although he did not promote historical research in the biblical field to the extent which his more liberal contemporary, William Newton Clarke, did at The Hamilton Theological Seminary (later called The Colgate Theological Seminary). While Strong believed that Christians should gain insights into truth from all fields of truth, he maintained that the ultimate measurement of truth was an authoritative revelation from God. Clarke, on the other hand, sought to interpret divine revelation in terms of human experience, as though God were revealing himself solely through the experience of mankind.[7]

In the field of theology he wrote such books as the famous *Systematic Theology* (1886), enlarged in three volumes in 1907-09; *Philosophy and Religion* (1888); *Christ in Creation and Ethical Monism* (1899); *The Great Poets and Their Theology* (1897); and *American Poets and Their Theology* (1916).

As an interpreter of God, he gave himself devotedly for forty years to the training of interpreters of the gospel. As president of Rochester Theological Seminary, he regarded himself as the "servant of the churches." He never indulged in the concept of a seminary as an ivory tower in which students and faculty would live in the rarified atmosphere of abstract research and purely academic pursuits. He felt too strongly the sacred responsibility of a theological institution to the churches. Because he believed devoutly that young men who were sent forth into the ministry should have a message to preach that was true to the New Testament, he expected that his teachers would have deep convictions and a sense of mission. In his own lectures, he manifested a tenacity of conviction, for he believed that a teacher must reach definite conclusions. But he always allowed a wholesome freedom in which the faculty members might do their work.

As an administrator, he never sought to override the judgment of his faculty. He was ever generous with his praise. And even in matters of discipline, he wore a velvet glove when exercising his authority. On one occasion, the faculty found it necessary to discipline a student by requiring a public

[7] *Dictionary of American Biography,* Vol. XVIII, pp. 142-43.

apology, as a condition of his remaining in school. At the first chapel after the Christmas holidays, President Strong introduced him as though he were a distinguished visitor with the words: "Mr. L. wishes to say a few words to us." [8]

Strong had found, upon coming to the seminary presidency, a faculty of seven men. Before his retirement in 1912, he had increased this number to fifteen. He had found almost nothing by way of a library. Forty years later there were 39,000 volumes, a full-time librarian with a staff of assistants, and permanent endowment funds amounting to $127,000. The German Department, which trained young men for the German Baptist Conference, received his warm encouragement. Always he urged its graduates to pursue further work in the English Department. In this he was eminently successful.[9]

As a teacher, Dr. Strong impressed his students with his tireless search for truth. He insisted upon classical training, regarding breadth as important as depth. To his mind, all fields of knowledge and of the arts could be of service in the interpretation of the Word of God. He himself "swept the whole field of philosophy and religion." He impressed his students that he always had power in reserve.[10] From him they learned the meaning of consecrated scholarship.

But perhaps his most human quality as a teacher, and that which left the deepest impression upon two generations of ministers, was his sympathy with and faith in young men. In the fall of 1903, for example, one student returned to school on crutches as the result of an injured hip incurred in an accident in California. At once he sent the boy to a specialist, paid for a steel splint which was necessary, and later on saw him through a nervous breakdown.[11]

In 1911, Professor Walter Rauschenbusch read a humorous paper at the annual banquet of the seminary to memorialize President Strong's concern for the placement of "his boys," as he liked to call them. It was entitled "Mr. Dooley on the Seminary."

[8] *Augustus Strong Memorial Number,* p. 15.
[9] *Ibid.,* pp. 24-27.
[10] *Ibid.,* p. 19.
[11] S. Fraser Langford, "The Gospel of Augustus H. Strong and Walter Rauschenbusch," *The Chronicle,* Vol. XIV, No. 1 (Jan., 1951), p. 9.

The churches they keep callin' him on the telephone like this: "Hello! Yes, deacon, is this you?" he sez. "Have I got any likely young colts this season? Sure, I have," he sez. "What would you be after wantin' now," he sez, "a high stepper for the Baptist buggy, or a safe one to plough a young orchard? All right, deacon," he sez. "I'll send him down for inspection, but rimimber my colts like oats for their feed, and they all like to trot in double harness. Goodbye." And before ye know, he's closed out the whole lot, and is riddy for another stock. So that's why the byes love their Prisident, for he's been like a father to thim. It's Dr. Sthrong, first in the Church, first in the town, and first in the hearts of the Siminary byes.[12]

His interest in the field of education surpassed the confines of seminary training. For example, he was a trustee of Vassar College from 1884 to 1918, and chairman of its board from 1906 to 1911. He participated in the movement which resulted in the new University of Chicago, established in 1890 to replace the original institution which had been forced to close its doors three years earlier for lack of funds. His role seems to have been that of arousing the interest of John D. Rockefeller in the plans. Actually, Dr. Strong had envisioned the erection of a Baptist university in New York city, with opportunities for research which did not exist at the time. It was in this scheme that he first tried to interest Mr. Rockefeller. He published a pamphlet which called attention to the tendency in Europe and America toward great centers of population as the foci of educational enterprise. He felt the need for more higher education under Baptist auspices. A further influence which he exerted was to introduce William Rainey Harper, the great Baptist scholar and administrator, to Mr. Rockefeller. Although the idea of a center in New York city was abandoned, for Columbia University had come in to meet the need, the enthusiasm and vision of Augustus Strong combined with the influence of Thomas W. Goodspeed of Morgan Park Seminary near Chicago and Frederick T. Gates of the American Baptist Education Society to secure Mr. Rockefeller's support for the refounding of the University of Chicago. To Dr. Strong must go the credit for having been the first to plant the idea of the university in Mr. Rockefeller's mind.[13]

---

[12] *Augustus Strong Memorial Number,* p. 20.
[13] *Dictionary of American Biography,* Vol. XVIII, pp. 142-43.

One further word needs to be said about Augustus Strong as an interpreter of God, and it concerns the direction which he gave to the thinking of the denomination for nearly half a century. This he accomplished in several ways. In the first place, in his capacity as seminary president and professor, he was a molder of ministers. During his administration, the seminary furnished more than seven hundred pastors throughout the country, and more than one hundred missionaries to other lands. Of these graduates, some became outstanding leaders of the denomination. The executive secretaries of the foreign, home, and publication societies claimed Rochester Theological Seminary as their alma mater. Sixty-five presidents or professors in Baptist educational institutions had received their training at Rochester.[14]

In the second place, Dr. Strong always made it a point to attend denominational meetings whether or not he had a part on the program. He was especially faithful to the Monroe Association. In this connection, a humorous anecdote is told about President Strong, Professor Stevens, and Professor True being obliged to walk all the way from Rochester to the meeting place of the association (several miles away)—all because four seminary students had appropriated the carriage which had been sent for them. The abashed students explained later that they had thought that the carriage had been sent for *them*. And, to make matters worse, the driver insisted that he could not tell professors from students![15]

For several years in the late eighties, Strong was a member of the Board of the American Baptist Missionary Union (now known as the American Baptist Foreign Mission Society), and from 1892 to 1895 he was its president. When the Baptist Convention of North America was formed in 1905 to strengthen the Baptist witness on this continent, Dr. Strong was elected president because he could represent best the Baptists of the North, South, and Canada. In all of his denominational interests, he was devoted to the local churches. Many times, he traveled several hundred miles in order to save men and churches to the denomination.

[14] *Augustus Strong Memorial Number,* pp. 59-60.
[15] *Ibid.,* p. 29.

Strong also gave direction to the thinking of the denomination through the medium of his numerous books, which have been mentioned already. It is indicative of his consuming concern for the missionary enterprise of the denomination that his last volume should have been *A Tour of the Missions, Observations and Conclusions* (1918), which was his report on a world-wide tour of American Baptist mission fields.

When Dr. Strong died on November 29, 1921, he was survived by his wife, Marguerite Geraldine Gerrit Jones, whom he had married on January 1, 1915 (his first wife, Harriet Louise Savage, whom he had married on November 6, 1861, having died in 1914) and four daughters and two sons of his first marriage. He left the legacy of a life which had been built well into the ministry of eight hundred graduates and of countless Baptists who had been led into a richer understanding of their Christian faith by the clarity of his logic, the integrity of his exposition of the gospel, and the warmth of his personal devotion to Christ. Truly, he had fought a good fight; he had finished his course; he had kept the faith.

Walter Rauschenbusch:
Prophet of Social Righteousness

ON A SUMMER DAY in 1912, two men shared a quart of strawberries, some milk, and crackers on the lakefront in Chicago. One was Dr. Walter Rauschenbusch, a man of distinguished appearance marked by a Vandyke beard and penetrating eyes that compensated for his defective hearing. The other was a young man, Dores R. Sharpe, who had been his student and private secretary and who was to become his biographer in the years to follow. They had come from a meeting at which Rauschenbusch had delivered an address. In the midst of a delightful hour of relaxation and good fellowship, Rauschenbusch said abruptly to his companion, "How do you think of me and my work?" The other's reply came without hesitation, "I think of you as an evangelist and of your work as evangelism of the truest sort." With deep emotion and an unexpected gesture of affection, Rauschenbusch threw his arms about young Sharpe and said: "I have always wanted to be thought of in that way. Your testimony gives me new fighting power. I have always regarded my public work as a form of evangelism, which called for a deeper repentance and a new experience of God's salvation." [1]

The incident affords a glimpse into the heart of the man who was even then the acknowledged leader of social Christianity in America. He was truly a prophet of social righteousness. His soul-consuming theme was always "the kingdom of God." In it he combined the personal devotion of a saint with the social zeal of a reformer. In the words of an admirer, "He was an Old Testament prophet come to life in our own day." [2]

His influence was great indeed. It gave rise to the quickening of social concern in American Protestantism. Through his

[1] Dores R. Sharpe, *Walter Rauschenbusch.* New York: The Macmillan Co., 1942, pp. 393-94.
[2] S. Fraser Langford, "The Gospel of Augustus H. Strong and Walter Rauschenbusch," *The Chronicle,* XIV, 1, p. 15.

personal contacts, his teaching, and his writing, he directed the thinking of a host of Christian leaders away from an exclusively individualistic concept of the gospel to an awareness of the implications of the teachings of Jesus for society and the multiple problems of an industrialized and urbanized economy and culture. The impact of his leadership extended into public life, for great statesmen like Theodore Roosevelt and Woodrow Wilson sought his counsel concerning an adequate program of social reform for the nation. At Rochester Theological Seminary he exerted his greatest influence upon the students he taught by giving them a new sense of mission. President Augustus H. Strong said of him on one occasion, "No more chivalrous or loving spirit was ever born, except our Lord and Redeemer." [3]

One may well inquire, therefore, into the wellspring from which sprang the genius of Walter Rauschenbusch, whose thought and labors were so largely responsible for the crystallization of the "social gospel" emphasis in American Protestantism. He himself never used the term "social gospel," until the writing of his last book, *A Theology for the Social Gospel,* which was published in 1917, the year before his death.

On April 15, 1865, the day following the assassination of President Lincoln, Walter Rauschenbusch as a five-year-old boy was seen hanging crepe on the door of a modest home in Rochester, New York. He was helping his parents participate in the mourning of their community for the dead President. On July 25, 1918, a tall, slender man, his red beard streaked with gray, his body cancered, his heart broken by the tragedy of world conflict, "stepped through the 'little postern gate' to be with God." [4] This was the span of life during which the forces of a rapidly changing world were buffeting his sensitive nature and challenging his alert mind to find the Christian solution to the problems which they brought in their wake.

Before he had reached his tenth birthday, the first transcontinental railroad had been completed. During his youth he saw the advent of such marvelous inventions as the refrigerating machine, the telephone, and the incandescent light. Before his

[3] Sharpe, *op. cit.,* p. 422.
[4] *Ibid.,* p. 1.

very eyes, a nation was being transformed from a rural to an industrial economy. As a student he observed how Darwinian evolution and German scholarship were combining to challenge the traditional interpretations of the Bible. He came under the influence also of liberal social thought that was encouraging a reorientation of the public mind to the social and economic problems created by the industrial revolution.

Rauschenbusch was born on October 4, 1861, within two short blocks of Rochester Theological Seminary, where his father, Professor August Rauchenbusch, taught for over thirty years and where many years later he himself was to teach. He was descended from Westphalian ancestors, the first of whom is supposed to have come from Sweden with Gustavus Adolphus to defend the Protestant cause during the Thirty Years' War. It was his father who transplanted the family to American soil and left Lutheranism for Baptist principles. As a matter of fact, August Rauschenbusch came to America to be somewhat of a missionary pastor to the immigrants from his homeland.

Walter's early schooling was at Barmen, Germany, where his mother had taken the three children of the family for an extended visit from 1866 to the spring of 1869. While there, he attended regularly a Baptist church and Sunday school. Upon their return home in August, 1869, Walter was enrolled in Pfafflin's Private School in Rochester and later at the Free Academy, where he received a classical training. During summers, he worked on a farm in Lycoming County in Pennsylvania. He received only twenty-five cents a day and very little to eat. His lifelong opposition to long hours of oppressive toil dated from this boyhood experience.

Very early the boy manifested the independence of thought in religious matters which characterized his entire life. On one occasion his father threatened to expel him from Sunday school for his heretical views. He had a passionate love of nature and of all living things.

His first deep soul experience came at about the age of seventeen. He explained later that it was a tender and mysterious response to his prayer for God's help in the problems of growing up. His baptism and graduation from the Free Academy came in close succession. Shortly thereafter, he left for his second trip to Europe.

From 1879 to 1883 he studied and traveled abroad. When an uncle offered to finance his way through a law course, he refused in favor of the ministry. When he completed his studies at the Evangelical Gymnasium of Gütersloh in Westphalia in 1883, he attended lectures for a few months at the University of Berlin where he heard some of the greatest biblical and theological scholars of the day. After a quick visit to England, he returned to Rochester to enter simultaneously the senior year of the university and the junior year of the seminary.

During the summer of 1884 he accepted a temporary pastorate in a small German Baptist Church in Louisville, Kentucky. His congregation almost doubled in three months, and there were many conversions. It was for him a wonderful experience. The next year he returned for a second summer. It was at this time that he wrote in his diary a statement which opens a window into his thinking:

> I don't believe that when a man believes in the vicarious death of Christ that death will be imputed to him; how can it? But if he begins to live a Christlike life, he will find that tho' there is no cross for him to be nailed to, he will die piecemeal by self-sacrifice just as Christ did even before his crucifixion and then he is at one with Christ and placed by God into the same category.[5]

He gave further indication of the independence of his thought and the deep desire which he felt for truth in the commencement oration which he delivered May 19, 1886, on "The Ethics of Thinking." He said in part:

> Others shrink from speaking out the new truth because they dread the consequences, not for themselves, but for others. For what truth has ever been born into this world without agony? The new cannot live except by destroying the old. . . . Today Christ comes not to bring peace, but the sword. . . . Well may the man whom God has commissioned to proclaim his purer truth to men, shrink from sowing the wind, lest he reap the whirlwind. But he dare not desist. . . . It is unbelief, it is atheism, on the part of the thinker to withhold from men a truth which he knows is from God, because he, forsooth, thinks it may wreck the world.[6]

[5] Sharpe, *op. cit.*, p. 55.
[6] *Ibid.*, p. 57.

During his seminary course, Rauschenbusch had experienced a second soul shake-up. Thereafter he no longer just "wished to preach and save souls," but resolved that in order to preach, he must live literally by the teachings and spirit of Jesus.[7] Out of such a decision, he volunteered for foreign missionary service. The American Baptist Foreign Mission Society at first considered sending him to India as president of the Telugu Theological Seminary at Ramapatnam, but their final decision was that he should first have a few years of pastoral work. It seems that his Old Testament professor had objected to his liberal views concerning the Old Testament. The Board possibly reasoned that experience in the pastorate might temper the intellectual views of the young theolog.

This disappointment was followed by another, when a strong church in Springfield, Illinois, withdrew a call to Rauschenbusch, apparently for the same reason. On June 1, 1886, however, he became pastor of the Second German Baptist Church in New York, a poverty-stricken congregation situated in the west side of the city on the border of "Hell's Kitchen."

It was in an old-fashioned and ugly building in a tough neighborhood, with a congregation of between one hundred fifty and two hundred, that Rauschenbusch began a ministry of eleven years which was to change the emphasis of his message. He began at a salary of nine hundred dollars a year, three hundred of which went for rent of a five-room flat. During his entire ministry there, he never received more than thirteen hundred dollars a year. As he worked among the tenement dwellers, he felt the poverty, the malnutrition, and the waste of life which stalked them constantly. He came to realize that conditions in the city were so bad that it was not a safe place for saved souls.

Almost from the start, he was influenced by Henry George, who was running at the time for mayor of New York. He joined forces with him and worked for his election as an alternative to the injustice which he had come to see in the economic system of his day. He worked also with Jacob Riis to secure playgrounds for children.

In the face of opposition from those who urged him "to leave

[7] *Ibid.*

social work and get back to Christian work," he began to study the Old Testament and the teachings of Jesus to see if he were wrong. But the more he plumbed the teachings of the Bible, the more he became convinced that the basic theme of the gospel is the "kingdom of God." It was just at this point that he discovered the synthesis "between the gospel for the individual and a gospel big enough to redeem the whole social system." [8] Should not God's will be done on earth as it is done in heaven? That was the question which confronted him. And the rest of his life was spent in an effort to answer it in the affirmative. Whereas prior to 1886 he had been reading sermons by Dwight L. Moody, Edward Judson, Alexander MacLaren, and Henry Drummond dealing with the Christian's personal problems, he now undertook a serious study of social issues. He read greedily the writings of Jacob Riis, Bellamy, Henry George, Tolstoi, Mazzini, Theodore Roosevelt, John A. Ryan, Paul Sabatier, Thomas á Kempis, William Allen White, Jane Addams, Henry Ward Beecher, William Jennings Bryan, John Calvin, David Lloyd George, J. W. Jenks, and a host of others who manifested a deep social concern.

During the winter of 1888 he fell prey to Russian grippe. Because he left his bed too soon to return to his pastoral duties, he suffered a relapse which resulted in a catarrhal condition that cost him his hearing. This misfortune pursued him for the rest of his life, causing him deep loneliness and, some say, the loss of the presidency of Rochester Theological Seminary. Yet he carried on his ministry with admirable courage and marked success. Within the first three years of his ministry, the church membership was almost doubled and new property was acquired. By 1891 he felt free to spend a few months of vacation in Europe.

During the years in New York, he linked friendship with two kindred spirits, Leighton Williams, pastor of Amity Baptist Church, and Nathaniel Schmidt, pastor of the Swedish Baptist Church. Together, they entered upon a study of the complex social issues of the day. Since 1887 Rauschenbusch had been expressing his social theories by means of articles in newspapers and religious journals, and by means of lectures. In 1889 he

[8] *Ibid.*, p. 62.

became a partner with Elizabeth Post, J. E. Raymond, and Leighton Williams in founding *For the Right,* a paper for the working people. It was not to be a political organ, but was intended to emphasize the need for a combination of personal regeneration and social reform. Through the years of publication, it was a distinctly Christian enterprise.

It was out of such a background of concern that the Brotherhood of the Kingdom came into existence in 1892. Its inception was inspired largely by Rauschenbusch, although Samuel Zane Batten, pastor of the Manayunk Baptist Church in Philadelphia, seems to have suggested the need for such an organization. At any rate, the idea was first explored in Philadelphia during the May Anniversaries of the Baptist Missionary Societies. Others present were Leighton Williams, George Dana Boardman, pastor of the First Baptist Church in Philadelphia, and William Newton Clarke and Nathaniel Schmidt of Hamilton Theological Seminary. In July there was a second meeting in New York. The final meeting for organization was held in December in the office of *The National Baptist,* a weekly published in Philadelphia.

The gathering place of the Brotherhood for twenty years was the beautiful farm of Leighton Williams' father in the hills beyond Marlboro-on-the-Hudson. For these sessions, Rauschenbusch and Williams prepared papers for discussion. It was a varied group. Batten was the fiery agitator; Schmidt, the biblical scholar; Clarke, the theologian; and Boardman, the advocate of church union. Of the several chapters of the Brotherhood which were established in other places, the one which met at Roger Babson's home in Wellesley Hills, near Boston, was the strongest.

In the course of the many discussions concerning the kingdom of God, Rauschenbusch pointed out that there were various views of the kingdom: the eschatological (that the kingdom will be in the life hereafter), the mystical (that the kingdom is within the believer), the millennial (that the reign of Christ will be established after the second coming of Christ), and the sociological (that the kingdom is a righteous social order). Rauschenbusch regarded all of these as defective. He felt that the kingdom of God is larger than anything contained in any of these views; he held that it includes the sum of all the divine and righteous forces in the world. He was particularly critical of the millennarian teaching, which he felt was based upon a narrow and unhistorical system of interpreting Scripture. He also attacked it for being a pessimistic flight from responsibility. It is little wonder that he incurred the intense opposition of the fundamentalists within Protestantism.

In 1897 Rauschenbusch and his wife, the former Pauline Rother, a Milwaukee schoolteacher whom he had married four years before, moved to Rochester. He had accepted a faculty post in the German Department of Rochester Theological Seminary, which he held until 1902 when he became professor of church history in the English Department. His deafness, which confined him to the lecture method, did not impair his influence as a teacher, for he breathed life into the facts of history, and made the subject a living thing. Although never dogmatic, he always taught for a verdict. From the first, he enjoyed a free hand in his department. This was by agreement with President Strong, who had made only one stipulation: that he always be careful to make things clear to his students so that they would not go away with false notions, and that he not upset the pastors of the churches.[9] During the stormy days when he came under attack by the fundamentalists and even by some members of the Board of Trustees, Strong stood by him. Although the president at times expressed the wish that Professor Rauschenbusch would make central the great doctrine of the believer's union with Christ, the warmest friendship and deepest respect continued between the two men.

In his capacity as historian, Rauschenbusch was essentially a sociologist with an appreciation of history. He paid little attention to the biographical in church history, being more interested in mass movements, great tendencies, and trends. The subjects which intrigued his interest most in this field were the historical development of premillennialism, the Anabaptist Movement, the history of Christian baptism, and American church history. When he offered a course one year on "The Devil," students humorously asked each other, "Are you going to go to the Devil with Rauchie?" It was a profitable elective; for in it he

---

[9] Sharpe, *Walter Rauschenbusch,* p. 156.

traced the history of the personalized conceptions of the principle of evil. It was another illustration of his use of history in the development of his ideas.

His writings were numerous. In 1901 he completed his father's autobiography under the title, *Das Leben von Augustus Rauschenbusch*. The next year he published a volume in German on the Civil Government of the United States, for the use of German-American youth in the schools. In 1907 he published the first of the books on social Christianity which made him famous. When he handed his manuscript copy for *Christianity and the Social Crisis* to the Macmillan Company, he sailed almost at once for Europe "with his tongue in his cheek." No one was more amazed at its reception than Rauschenbusch. He returned to find himself famous, and he was obliged to plunge into a grueling nine-months period of public lectures. In 1910 he preached the Annual Sermon at the Northern Baptist Convention meeting in Chicago and delivered the Earle Lectures at the Pacific School of Religion on the west coast. His book had come at the right moment. America was ripe for it in theological developments and economic thinking. A cyclic business depression was taking place, and the "muck-raking" revelations of Lincoln Steffens, Ida Tarbell, and others had aroused the public mind on social issues.

In 1910 a little volume appeared which revealed the inner spiritual quality of the man more than any other book. It was entitled *For God and the People; Prayers of the Social Awakening*. Most indicative of his depth of spirit is what he called "The Author's Prayer":

O Thou who art the light of my soul, I thank Thee for the incomparable joy of listening to Thy voice within, and I know that no word of Thine shall return void, however brokenly uttered. If aught in this book was said through lack of knowledge, or through weakness of faith in Thee or of love for sin, I pray Thee to overrule my sin and turn aside its force before it harm Thy cause. Pardon the frailty of Thy servant, and look upon him only as he sinks his life in Jesus, his Master and Saviour.[10]

This was followed in 1912 by *Christianizing the Social Order*, which represents the crystallization of Rauschenbusch's thinking

[10] Cited in Sharpe, *op. cit.*, p. 282.

on social problems and the message of Christianity in relation
to them. In it he sets forth the proposition that the realm of
business and industry is the unredeemed section of the social
order in America. He outlines the fundamental demands of a
Christian economic order as justice, collective property rights,
democracy, approximate equality, and co-operation.

His last and most mature book, the product of thirty years of
experience, was *A Theology for the Social Gospel,* published in
1917. It grew out of the Nathaniel W. Taylor Foundation
Lectures at Yale School of Religion for that year. Here, for the
first time, he used the term "social gospel." The book reflects
a concern that what had come to be known as the "social gospel"
was growing ever thinner in theological content and bordering
on the purely humanistic approach to the problems of society.
Thus he sought to undergird the movement with a Christian
theology. His basic contention was that the kingdom of God,
which was central in Jesus' teaching, had become displaced in
the historical development of Christianity by the idea of the
church. While he did not deny the validity of the church, he
felt that it existed for the advancement of the kingdom or rule
of God. He wanted men to get back to the heart of Jesus'
message, which was the preaching of the kingdom of God in the
power of the Spirit. His interpretation of the death of Christ
was an interesting departure from the traditional views on the
atonement. He saw the public sins of organized society (religious bigotry, graft and political power, corruption of justice,
mob spirit, and militarism) as the cause of the Savior's death,
not the specific sins of any one individual.

In his theology he did not deny the importance of the personal relationship of the believer to Jesus Christ. He insisted
always upon the importance of regeneration and personal faith.
His conception of missions, for example, was evangelical. He
warned against substituting what he called secondary conceptions of missions, such as the fostering of secular education,
philanthropic efforts, or the spread of denominational propa-
ganda. The central aim of missions, he insisted, was "the extension of faith in the crucified and risen Christ, who imparts
His spirit to those who believe in Him and thereby redeems
them from the domination of the flesh and the world and their

corruption, and transforms them into spiritual beings, conformed to His likeness and partaking of His life." [11] It was not the denial of the redemptive character of Christianity which marked his theology, but the shifting of the central position of emphasis from the doctrine of the personal and mystical union of believers in Christ, without rejecting it, to the doctrine of the kingdom of God as the way of life for the community of believers as they live corporately in the world. This he did as a corrective to the general emphasis upon the personal aspect of the Christian religion.

In his political thought, Rauschenbusch saw in Christian Socialism the solution to the economic and political ills of society. Yet he never joined the Socialist Party. And he was always opposed to the Marxian cataclysmic approach to the ills of mankind. He did not believe in socializing everything, but only the large-scale means of production. He had a profound faith in progress and the possibility of gradual change under Christian influence.

His views on war underwent development during his lifetime. In 1898 he lauded the Spanish-American War. By 1910 he had developed a philosophy against most wars, although he still approved of force as the *ultima ratio*. He never isolated war as an evil by itself, but saw it as a phenomenon growing out of unjust social conditions. This undoubtedly is one of the major reasons for his unwillingness to take sharp sides in the First World War. His dislike of British imperialism and his basic lack of sympathy with English policies colored his views on the conflict. It was not until a few weeks before his death that he wrote a letter, at the urging of his friend, Dr. Cornelius Woelfkin, indicating that he regarded Germany as guilty. It was thought by some of his friends that his death on July 25, 1918, was due not only to the ravages of cancer, but also to a broken heart caused by witnessing, during the war years, the negation of all that he had taught.

Were Rauschenbusch here today, he would be gratified to see that American Protestantism is more alert than ever before to

---

[11] From an article on "Conception of Missions" in *The Watchman* (New York, Nov. 24, 1892) cited in Vernon P. Bodien, *The Social Gospel of Walter Rauschenbusch and Its Relation to Religious Education.* (New Haven, 1944), pp. 44-45.

the responsibility of the churches to exert social as well as individual action in the continuous struggle against sin. His ministry has exerted a profound influence in a period of great social and economic change.

To reflect upon the greatness of Walter Rauschenbusch and upon his limitations is to realize afresh the wisdom of God in entrusting his gospel to the church, rather than to any one person. For prophets may come and make their contribution and pass away, but the continuing witness of the great company of believers of all ages provides the mosaic in which we see the fullness of God's design. If we had known only Augustine or Luther or Calvin or Jonathan Edwards or John Wesley or Walter Rauschenbusch, how poor we should be! But having known them all and having received the special contribution and corrective influence of each, how rich we are in the heritage of our faith and life!

A Manual

on

Ordination, Licensing, and Ministerial Listing

Prepared under the direction of the Ministers Council, the National Council of American Baptist Men, the State and City Executives, and the Seminary Presidents of the American Baptist Convention.

An Introductory Word

Because of the wide divergence in practices of ordination to the Gospel Ministry throughout the territory of the American Baptist Convention and the difficulties arising therefrom, a Committee on Ordination Standards and Procedure was appointed by a joint committee of Seminary Presidents and State and City Secretaries to study the whole question of ordination and to prepare a statement which might be adopted by each State Convention and City Mission Society as a standard to be attained and a procedure to be followed.

Beginning in 1942, following the democratic process, numerous drafts and revisions were made until the present *Manual on Ordination, Licensing, and Ministerial Listing* has been developed. This manual has been reviewed and approved by the following groups: the Ministers Council of the American Baptist Convention, the National Council of American Baptist Men, the State and City Secretaries, the Commission on the Ministry, the Board of Education and Publication, and the American Baptist Seminary Presidents.

We present these Standards and Procedures as a practical basis for the uniting of our interests and goals. This material has been widely distributed through two editions of a leaflet published by the Ministers Council and the National Council of American Baptist Men. We would urge State Conventions, City Mission Societies, and Associations to take the necessary action recommending this to our churches as standard procedure.

Ordination to the Baptist Ministry

When a Church has voted its approval of a man for ordination to the Christian Ministry, it has placed its stamp of approval on the man from the point of view of the local Church. In that the man will work, in his lifetime, with other Churches, and with a host of other ordained ministers, it is necessary that he conform to certain basic standards that the work of the Churches might progress on a high level. By following the standards herein set forth, he will have the approval of his fellow ministers, the National Council of American Baptist Men and of the American Baptist Convention.

If the candidate meets the Ordination Standards he will be granted an Ordination Certificate registered by number with the Ministers Council of the American Baptist Convention. This Certificate of Ordination will certify that he is a duly qualified and trained man.

By ordination, those who feel called of God to preach the "unsearchable riches of Christ" are set apart to important positions of responsibility and trust in pastoral and missionary leadership by a local Church, upon the advice of a duly called council of qualified representatives from the Churches. Ordination is a door which should be open *only* to the qualified and worthy.

Heretofore there has been an utter lack of uniformity in the important matter of standards for ordination among the Churches of the American Baptist Convention. Instances have been known where men who could not meet the qualifications of other denominations have found refuge in our fold. Men who have been forced to leave other denominations have found they could enter the Baptist Ministry. This has resulted in confusion and has worked a hardship on the Churches, Ministers, and on the work of the American Baptist Convention. It has produced a divisive influence on the work of Christ in our day.

In response to the demand for a uniform standard of ordination to the Baptist Ministry, the following standard was adopted at St. Louis in 1948 by the Executive Committee of the Ministers Council of the American Baptist Convention, and approved by the National Council of American Baptist Men.

I. Ordination Standards

1. A Candidate for ordination to the Gospel Ministry shall have had satisfactory service as a licensed preacher of the Gospel. He shall present acceptable testimony from the local Church and other reliable sources as to his moral character, integrity and Christian experience. A Candidate shall have at least a college degree and three years of theological training in a recognized institution of learning to qualify for ordination and for the recognized Certificate of Ordination.* (This is understood to include, in the case of graduates from non-Baptist Schools, a study of Baptist History, principles and polity, as well as a knowledge of the American Baptist Convention and its affiliated and co-operating societies and organizations.) He shall declare it to be his purpose to find his field of service within the American Baptist Convention, and to remain in full co-operation with other Churches in the State and National Conventions.

2. It is desirable that a Candidate for ordination shall have at least one year's previous experience in the Baptist Ministry, to prove his fitness for the work, and his loyalty to the denominational program. This need not apply to graduates of Baptist Seminaries who are recommended by recognized officials.

3. An ordained minister desiring to come into the Baptist denomination from another communion shall conform to section 1 (above). He shall present a letter of recommendation from the denomination from which he came, and have the recommendation of the Permanent Council, Association Committee, or the State Committee on the Ministry, as the case may be, and, further, be approved by a regularly called ordination council before he receives state-wide recognitions and privileges.

4. A Candidate for ordination should find himself in fellowship with and willing to co-operate with other Churches within the American Baptist Convention. He should be asked, as a matter of honor, to agree to return his ordination papers if he no longer finds it possible to maintain his loyalty.

* See the footnote on page 127.

II. Ordination Procedure

1. A Church desiring ordination for one of its members shall arrange for him to meet with the State, Associational or Permanent Council for interview and counsel (whichever is the recognized and regular procedure of the area). Prior to his meeting with the Committee he shall have submitted in writing the requirements requested in section I-1 and II-6.

2. The Candidate must be a member of the ordaining Church and should have a definite assignment to specific Christian service.

3. The Church must vote its own approval of the Candidate and vote to call a council (or refer to the permanent Council) for examination of the Candidate's qualifications for the Christian Ministry.

4. Each Church in the Association shall be invited to appoint the Pastor and two delegates, preferably Deacons, to the examining council. The State Ministers Council, the State Board and the State Permanent Council on Ordination, where one exists, should be invited to send a representative.

5. In order to be fair to the Candidate, to not prejudice the examining council, to give time to secure the regular ordination materials and plan the program properly, it is recommended that the ordination service be held not sooner than two weeks after the examination.

6. The Candidate shall be required to make a statement to the examining council, in writing, concerning:

(a) His Christian Experience.

(b) His call to the Ministry.

(c) His preparation for the Christian Ministry.

(d) His Christian beliefs.

(e) His knowledge and beliefs concerning Baptist History, polity, and principles.

(f) His personal attitude toward the denominational program.

(g) His loyalty to the American Baptist Convention and his promise to surrender his ordination papers if such loyalty ceases.

7. Duties of the Clerk of the Ordaining Church:

(*a*) Invite Pastor and two delegates from each Church of the Association.

(*b*) Invite a representative of the State Ministers Council, or the Permanent Council on Ordination.

(*c*) Secure from, or through the State Office, or the Ministers Council, the type of ordination certificate to which the Candidate is entitled by training.*

8. Duties of Clerk elected at time of Ordination:

(*a*) Keep minutes of the procedure.

(*b*) List visiting Pastors and delegates.

(*c*) Fill out questionnaire for the Registry of Ministers, as supplied by the Ministers and Missionaries Benefit Board.

(*d*) File copy of minutes with the ordaining Church, State Convention Office and the Ministers and Missionaries Benefit Board.

The Ordination Service

The significance which we attach to the act of ordination reflects the importance which we attach to the ministry itself. Since it is in our thought the "high calling," the induction of a candidate into it should be observed with carefulness and with a due solemnity. A service of ordination should be made one of the most impressive services which a church conducts. The parts which by long usage have come to be recognized in an ordination service lend themselves to impressiveness if they are seriously given. The following is a suggested order which may help a committee in preparing a service. The vows of ordination are included because we believe the increased use of this feature is to be commended.

* Ordination Certificate. The ordination certificate of the Ministers Council of the American Baptist Convention is only granted to candidates who have completed four years of college and three years of recognized theological training. It may be secured from the Secretary of the Ministers Council. It is numbered and registered with the Ministers Registry of the Ministers and Missionaries Benefit Board of the American Baptist Convention.

Any church may, upon inquiry, learn whether a candidate for a pulpit is so registered. If he is, the church has every assurance that the man is duly qualified from an educational point of view, and was regularly ordained.

INVOCATION
SCRIPTURE LESSON
SERMON
VOWS

TO THE CANDIDATE:

Will you, in obedience to the divine will, faithfully preach the gospel, tenderly minister to the needy, and with all diligence strive to extend the Kingdom of Christ throughout the earth?

I will do so, the Lord being my helper.

Will you remember constantly that you are a minister of the world-wide Church of Christ and endeavor to lead your people in service for the evangelizing of the world?

I will do so, the Lord being my helper.

Will you maintain and set forward, as much as lieth in you, quietness and peace among all people and especially among them that are or shall be committed to your care?

I will apply myself thereto, the Lord being my helper.

TO THE PEOPLE: (Members of the Church to Stand)

(This is to be used when the Ordination is in the Church to which the candidate has been called.)

Will you, the members of this church, uphold the hands of your minister as fellow workers with him for the furtherance of the Gospel? Will you honor him with your support, your sympathy and your co-operation that your communion and fellowship may be rich in joy and strength and fruitful of good works?

This we engage to do by the help of the Lord.

PRAYER OF ORDINATION
CHARGE TO THE CHURCH
CHARGE TO THE MINISTER
WELCOME AND RIGHT HAND OF FELLOWSHIP
BENEDICTION: By the Candidate

NOTES:

1. The Moderator of the Council should preside at the service.

2. The complete church minutes and the report of the Council should be carefully prepared and read at the opening of the service.

3. To guard against awkwardness, arrangements for the Ordination Prayer should be carefully made. It is usually better for a limited number to participate in the "Laying on of Hands."

Licensing

To some extent the practice of Licensing Ministers has been neglected among our churches in recent years. It should be revised and enlarged. When a young man gives evidence of gifts for the ministry he should be encouraged to exercise those gifts. Licensing of ministers should be a preliminary stage in their preparation and should take the place of premature ordination.

A candidate for licensing, therefore, should also meet the Association, City Mission Society, or State Committee on Ordination. He should be examined as to his experience and purpose in Christian work. If he possesses the proper qualifications he should be counseled as to his preparation and recommended to his church for licensing. There should be a Service of Recognition connected with the granting of the license, and it would also be well for the State Conventions and City Mission Societies to keep as complete a list as possible of all who are thus licensed. The license should be issued for a limited time subject to renewal. In this way it is possible to keep in closer touch with young men who are looking forward to the ministry.

Procedure of Licensing

We Recommend:

1. That for a period of Preparation and Experience necessary for Ordination, a Regular Procedure of Licensing be practiced to encourage young men of evident gifts for the ministry.

2. That the Regular Procedure of Licensing consist of the following:

(1) That, upon request of the Church, the candidate meet

the Association or City Mission Society Committee on Ordination for examination in Christian experience, purpose, and preparation.

(2) That, upon the recommendation of the Ordination Committee, the Church arrange a Service of Recognition for the candidate.

(3) That a Certificate of License be provided by the Church, which shall bear the signature of the Moderators and Clerks of the Association and Church, and presented to the candidate at the time of the Service of Recognition.

(4) That the License be issued for a limited time, the time limit to be set by the Committee when it is issued.

(5) That candidates thus licensed be considered eligible for the administration of Baptism, the Lord's Supper, and officiating at Funerals and Weddings, when compatible with the laws of the state, so long as he is acting as the regular pastor of a Baptist Church which has requested him so to do.

Listing Our Ministers

WE RECOMMEND:

That upon adoption by State or City Mission Society of the Standards and Procedure of Ordination and Procedure of Licensing, each State Convention and City Mission begin to keep the lists of their ministers in the following way:

(1) List I, to include all ministers who have met the required Standards and Procedure for Ordination and have been recognized as duly ordained.

(2) List II, to include all those who have not reached the minimum standards for ordination, and have nevertheless been ordained, by the regular procedure, after the adoption of the standards.

(3) List III, to include all ministers who have been Licensed according to the Procedure on Licensing, or whose names appeared in a State Convention Annual in the list of licensed ministers for that year.

(4) List IV, to include all others.

That each State Convention and City Mission Society refuse

to list any minister who refuses to give the information required for his proper listing.

That a form be provided which will facilitate getting all necessary information for listing the ministers of our Convention, and that each State Convention and City Mission Society use these forms.

That the following form be used to get the information for listing the ministers:

Ministerial Information Blank

Name_____Date of Birth_____
       last   first   middle

Address_____

Formal Education_____
        School or College   Degree   Date

_____
        Seminary   Degree   Date

Licensing Church_____

Date_____

Ordaining Church_____

Date_____

State Ordination Committee_____

Date_____

Association Ordination Committee_____

Date_____

Date when this was signed_____

Signature_____

NOTE: Reverse side of card must show the fields of service since entering the ministry, and approximate dates.

Distributed on behalf of the Convention
by
THE BOARD OF EDUCATION AND PUBLICATION
OF THE AMERICAN BAPTIST CONVENTION

A Selected Bibliography

Note: This list contains only those volumes which are reasonably accessible. For other resources, see footnotes in the text.

BODIEN, Vernon P., *The Social Gospel of Walter Rauschenbusch and Its Relation to Religious Education.* New Haven: The Yale University Press, 1944. ix, 169 pp.

COMMAGER, Henry S., *The American Mind: An Interpretation of American Thought and Character Since the 1880's.* New Haven: The Yale University Press, 1950. ix, 476 pp.

deBLOIS, Austen K., *The Making of Ministers.* Philadelphia: The Judson Press, 1936. vi, 276 pp. A History of The Eastern Baptist Theological Seminary, 1925-1935.

FLEMING, Sandford, *God's Gold; The Story of Baptist Beginnings in California, 1849-1860.* Philadelphia: The Judson Press, 1949. 216 pp.

HARTSHORNE, Hugh and Milton C. Froyd, *Theological Education in the Northern Baptist Convention.* Philadelphia: The Judson Press, 1945. 242 pp.

HERRICK, Everett C., *Turns Again Home: Andover Newton Theological School and Reminiscences from an Unkept Journal.* Boston: The Pilgrim Press, 1949. 202 pp.

HOVEY, George R., *Alvah Hovey, His Life and Letters.* Philadelphia: The Judson Press, 1928. 267 pp.

LAWRENCE, Matthew, *John Mason Peck: The Pioneer Missionary.* New York: Fortuny's Co., 1940. 118 pp.

MANSON, T. W., *The Church's Ministry.* London: Hodder & Stoughton, 1948. 112 pp.

MAY, Mark A. *et al., The Education of American Ministers.* 4 volumes. New York: Institute of Social and Religious Research, 1934.

McGLOTHLIN, W. J., *Baptist Beginnings in Education: A History of Furman University.* Nashville: Sunday School Board of Southern Baptist Convention, 1926. 249 pp.

OLSON, Adolf and Virgil A., *Seventy-five Years: A History of Bethel Theological Seminary, St. Paul, Minn., 1871-1946.* Chicago: Baptist Conference Press, 1946. 232 pp.

PAYNE, Ernest A., *The First Generation.* London: Carey Press, 1936. 143 pp.

REID, Ira De A., *The Negro Baptist Ministry: An Analysis of Its Profession, Preparation and Practices.* Report of Survey conducted by the Joint Survey Commission of the Baptist Inter-Convention Committee (American Bapist Convention, National Baptist Convention, Inc., Southern Baptist Convention). A mimeographed copy of the report as submitted to the Committee for study and publication.

ROBINSON, H. Wheeler, *The Life and Faith of the Baptists.* Revised Edition. London: The Kingsgate Press, 1946. ix, 158 pp.

SHARPE, Dores R., *Walter Rauschenbusch.* New York: The Macmillan Co., 1942. xiii, 463 pp.

SWEET, William W., *Religion on the American Frontier: The Baptists, 1783-1830.* New York: Henry Holt & Co., 1931. ix, 652 pp. A valuable collection of source materials, prefaced by several interpretive chapters.

TORBET, Robert G., *A History of the Baptists.* Philadelphia: The Judson Press, 1950. 538 pp.

UNDERWOOD, A. C., *A History of the English Baptists.* London: Union Publication Dept. (Kingsgate Press), 1947. 286 pp.

WEIS, Frederick L., *The Colonial Churches and the Colonial Clergy of the Middle and Southern Colonies, 1607-1776.* Lancaster, Mass.: Society of the Descendants of the Colonial Clergy, 1938. 140 pp.

——————————, *The Colonial Clergy and Colonial Churches of New England.* Lancaster, Mass.: Society of the Descendants of the Colonial Clergy, 1936. 280 pp.

WOODSON, Hortense, *Giant in the Land: A Biography of William Bullein Johnson, First President of the Southern Baptist Convention.* Nashville: Broadman Press, 1950. xii, 164 pp.

Date Due